MEDICAL OFFICE PROFESSIONALS

PRACTICAL CAREER GUIDES

Series Editor: Kezia Endsley

Dental Assistants and Hygienists, by Kezia Endsley
Health and Fitness Professionals, by Kezia Endsley
Medical Office Professionals, by Marcia Santore

MEDICAL OFFICE PROFESSIONALS

A Practical Career Guide

MARCIA SANTORE

ROWMAN & LITTLEFIELD
Lanham • Boulder • New York • London

Published by Rowman & Littlefield
An imprint of The Rowman & Littlefield Publishing Group, Inc.
4501 Forbes Boulevard, Suite 200, Lanham, Maryland 20706
www.rowman.com

6 Tinworth Street, London, SE11 5AL, United Kingdom

British Library Cataloguing in Publication Information Available

Library of Congress Cataloging-in-Publication Data

Names: Santore, Marcia, 1960– author.
Title: Medical office professionals : a practical career guide / Marcia Santore.
Description: Lanham : Rowman & Littlefield, 2019. | Series: Practical career guide | Includes bibliographical references.
Identifiers: LCCN 2018042070 (print) | LCCN 2018043180 (ebook) | ISBN 9781538111888 (Electronic) | ISBN 9781538111871 (pbk. : alk. paper)
Subjects: LCSH: Medical personnel—Vocational guidance | Allied health personnel—Vocational guidance.
Classification: LCC R690 (ebook) | LCC R690 .S26 2019 (print) | DDC 610.73/7069—dc23
LC record available at https://lccn.loc.gov/2018042070

Printed in the United States of America

Contents

Introduction

There are many opportunities in healthcare, from entry level to advanced practice.

So You Want a Career as a Medical Office Professional

- Do you like the idea of helping other people while you earn a good living?
- Do you work well as part of a team?
- Can you deal with a fast-paced environment where you might have to respond quickly?
- Are you patient and empathetic with other people?
- Do you want to work in a growing field with room for advancement?
- Do you want a job that's fulfilling and important?

If you answered *yes* to these questions, a career as a medical office professional might be for you!

There is a lot of joy and satisfaction in helping people maintain their health, get well, or manage a chronic health issue. Working in healthcare is a way to do good while doing well—that is, helping others in a job that pays well. The healthcare professions are growing—every career covered in this career guide is growing at a rate that's well above the national average for jobs.

This career guide will give you an overview of the many types of healthcare careers available. There are different education and certification requirements, and different salaries to match. In the next section, we'll cover a few of the healthcare jobs that are out there and talk to people who are in those jobs right now:

- Nurse practitioner
- Physician assistant
- Health information technician
- Optometrist
- Pharmacy technician
- Phlebotomist
- Sonographer
- Surgical technologist

In the following chapters, you can learn more about how to pursue the education you'll need for a career in healthcare, and how to apply for and interview for the job of your dreams.

SUCCESS IN A HEALTHCARE CAREER

To be successful in any of these healthcare careers, keep the issues discussed in the following sections in mind.

Be a People Person

That means putting your patients first and remembering that patients are people first. Some patients are great—smiling, friendly, happy to forgive small mistakes. But people who are ill or in pain may be grumpy, rude, or uncooperative. As a healthcare professional, you need to treat patients and their families/caregivers with compassion and empathy. Think about how you would feel in their situation and treat them the way you would want to be treated.

TEN TIPS TO A GREAT BEDSIDE MANNER

1. *Pay attention.* Show the patient that you're paying attention. Don't fill in forms, text, or answer the phone.

2. *Listen.* Patients tell stories to explain what's going on with their health. Good listening helps avoid mistakes that come from making assumptions.

3. *Look.* Make eye contact and greet patients in an appropriately friendly way. Let them know they are recognized as human beings first, not just an illness or an injury. Watch their body language—it's an important part of communicating how they're feeling.

4. *Be aware of touch.* Medical care often involves a lot of touching. Some patients don't mind, but others find this intrusive. Or being touched might make their condition more painful. Be aware of how your patient is responding to touch.

5. *Respect privacy.* It can be uncomfortable and embarrassing for patients to have to take off their clothes or answer intimate questions during a medical visit. Be sure they have sufficient privacy to change or to talk about sensitive topics without being overheard.

6. *Don't Be Judgy.* Sometimes you'll have a patient who you don't like or who you think is responsible for their own situation. Remember that you don't know their whole story. Patients have the right to be treated with dignity, not disapproval. It's your job to show—in your tone of voice and your body language—that they are safe and they can trust you.

7. *Talk Like a Person.* Don't use a lot of medical jargon when you're talking to a patient. They won't be impressed, but they could misunderstand something important. Use positive language.

8. *Be Trustworthy.* Deserve your patients' trust by always being honest and truthful, maintain confidentiality, keep your promises, and always check before sharing patient information—don't assume you know who can see what.

9. *Be Kind.* Be considerate and caring. Put yourself in the patient's place—how would you want to be treated? Assume the best about everyone you encounter—patients, families, and your colleagues.

10. *Be Responsible.* Good patient care also involves being professional, looking professional, being on time, and going the extra mile when your patients need you.

WILMA HYDE: PEDIATRIC NURSE PRACTITIONER

Wilma Hyde. *Courtesy of Wilma Hyde*

Wilma Hyde, APRN, is a pediatric nurse practitioner with Plymouth Pediatrics/Speare Memorial Hospital in Plymouth, New Hampshire. She received her bachelor's degree in nursing from Northeastern University and her master's degree from Simmons College, both in Boston. Her patients know her as a warm, caring, intelligent, and knowledgeable practitioner. She is also an active member of the community, and has served in many roles, including school board member and health advocate.

What is a typical day in your job?

Nurse practitioners work in a variety of settings and have different levels of independence depending on what state they are licensed in. My setting is a rural pediatric clinic in New Hampshire. A typical day for me would range from seeing patients in the office to attending a delivery to rounding on a patient in our small community hospital to providing phone advice after hours. Nurse practitioners provide primary care that includes physicals, treatment of illness, prescribing medications, and referrals as appropriate. In New Hampshire, APRNs have full autonomy and can diagnose, prescribe, and treat independently. After twenty-plus years at this job, there is never a boring day!

What is the best part of your job?

Giving good care. Feeling like I made a difference. Getting a hug. Seeing the result of good care. Making a difference in people's lives.

What is the most surprising thing about your job?

How wide a range of knowledge is necessary to do the job well.

What's next? Where do you see yourself going from here?

Training the next generation! Becoming more politically active. And participating in leadership to ensure that my clinic will survive and thrive.

Did your education prepare you for the job?

Education provides you with the skills to be a critical thinker, access information, be curious, and interpret information. Being a pediatric nurse prior to going on to become a pediatric nurse practitioner has given me a strong foundation to build from. Ongoing continuing education is expected daily (in the form of research for evidence-based care) as well as in the form of continuing educational conferences/podcasts/reading. It's a never-ending journey of learning and growth.

Is the job of nurse practitioner what you expected it to be?

I actually began my career as a neonatal nurse practitioner (caring for critically ill newborns) and ended up in outpatient pediatric primary care due to a move to be closer to my (at that time, new) husband. I thought I would try it out, and here I am—twenty-one years later!

Be a Team Player

Everyone in the medical office works as part of a team. So it's super important to be able and willing to communicate with your team members. You'll need to know the right medical terminology and how and when to use it. Ask questions when you need to, and give answers when someone asks you a question. Another important part of being a team player is to treat all your coworkers with respect. Every medical office has a hierarchy. Some people will be above you, some will be at the same level, and some will be below you on that ladder. Regardless, always treat everyone you work with respectfully—think about how you would want them to treat you. And a little more of that compassion and empathy never hurts, either.

Keep Your Balance

Healthcare can get stressful. Of course, when an emergency comes up, everyone has to be able to respond quickly and do their part, without freaking out. But even when there is no immediate emergency, working in a medical office can be stressful and sometimes involves long hours, depending on your role. It's

EVEN MORE OPTIONS

Of course, we can't fit every possible healthcare career into one career guide. What you'll learn in this book about the world of healthcare professions can apply to more than just the eight great jobs we've included here. Some other options for a healthcare career might include:

- Athletic trainer
- Audiologist
- Biological technician
- Biomedical engineer
- Cardiovascular technologist and technician
- Chiropractor
- Clinical director
- Clinical laboratory technician
- Critical care nurse
- Dental assistant
- Dental hygienist
- Dentist
- Diagnostic medical sonographer
- Dietitian
- Emergency medical technician
- Genetic counselor
- Health and social services manager
- Health educator
- Healthcare administrator
- Healthcare manager
- Hearing aid specialist
- Home health aide
- Laboratory animal caretaker
- Laboratory technician
- Licensed practice/vocational nurse
- Massage therapist
- Medical administrative assistant
- Medical and health services manager
- Medical assistant
- Medical coder
- Medical equipment preparer
- Medical secretary
- Medical social worker
- Medical transcriptionist
- Mental health counselor
- MRI technologist
- Nuclear medicine technologist
- Nurse anesthetist
- Nurse midwife
- Nursing assistant
- Occupational health and safety specialist
- Occupational therapist
- Occupational therapy assistant
- Optician
- Orthotist/prosthetist
- Paramedic
- Personal care aide
- Pharmacist
- Physical therapist
- Physical therapist aide
- Physical therapist assistant
- Physician (so many kinds!)
- Psychiatric aide
- Psychologist
- Radiation therapist
- Radiologic technologists
- Recreational therapist
- Registered nurse
- Rehabilitation counselor
- Respiratory therapist
- Speech pathologist
- Substance abuse counselor
- Veterinarian
- Veterinary technologist/technician

important to be able to handle stress well so that you can keep doing your job to give the patients the best care possible. Dealing with stress means *actually paying attention to taking care of yourself.* So enjoy your time with family and friends, have outside hobbies, meditate, meet with a counselor if you need to, maintain your own health with healthful food and plenty of exercise— whatever works for you to keep that all-important work-life balance.

Keep Learning

Continuing education is part of working in healthcare. New medical techniques keep being invented. New drugs keep being discovered. New technologies for medicine, record keeping, etc. are invented or improved every week. And new rules and regulations change how patient care gets delivered. To provide the best care to their patients, healthcare workers keep up with the constant changes and maintain their certification by continuing their education. As a healthcare professional, you'll keep learning long after your official "schooling" ends. Continuing to learn is also the road to advancement in the healthcare field. You can earn further degrees and certification in order to move forward in your career.

1

Why Choose a Career in the Medical Professionals Field?

*I*n this chapter, you'll find an introduction to a few of the many healthcare jobs available in the United States. There's something for everyone here—start right from high school or earn an advanced degree; work directly with patients or behind the scenes. All are growing fields in need of people who are dedicated to helping others.

- Nurse practitioner
- Physician assistant
- Health information technician
- Optometrist
- Pharmacy technician
- Phlebotomist
- Sonographer
- Surgical technologist

Nurse Practitioner

WHAT IS A NURSE PRACTITIONER?

A nurse practitioner is a registered nurse (RN) with a graduate degree and advanced training in diagnosing and treating all kinds of patients. Nurse practitioners work directly with patients. They provide primary and preventive care. Most nurse practitioners work in a physician's office or outpatient healthcare facilities. Some work in hospitals or in specialized health practices. Check out the box "What Does a Nurse Practitioner Do?"

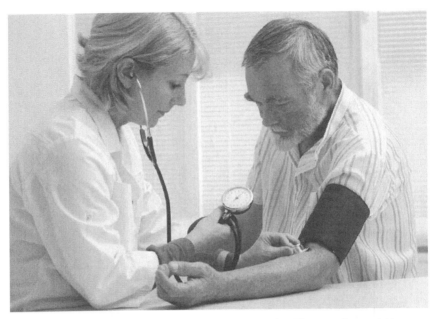

Nurse practitioners usually specialize in a particular type of healthcare, such as geriatrics.

WHAT DOES A NURSE PRACTITIONER DO?

- Provide primary or specialized care for patients
- Order, perform, and interpret diagnostic tests such as lab work and X-rays
- Diagnose and treat acute and chronic conditions such as diabetes, high blood pressure, infections, and injuries
- Prescribe medications and other treatments
- Manage patients' overall care
- Provide counseling
- Educate patients on disease prevention and positive health and lifestyle choices

Nurse practitioners are also known as advanced practice registered nurses (APRN). To be a nurse practitioner, you first need to be an RN with a bachelor's degree. Then you earn a master's degree with advanced training. Nurse practitioners generally focus on working with one kind of patient (such as children, adults, or older adults) or with one kind of medical problem (cancer, fertility, mental health, or sports medicine, for instance). You can be certified in more than one specialty (see the box "Nurse Practitioner Specialty Areas").

NURSE PRACTITIONER SPECIALTY AREAS

Specialties	Subspecialties
Acute care	Allergy and immunology
Adult health	Cardiovascular
Family health	Dermatology
Gerontology health	Emergency
Neonatal health	Endocrinology
Oncology	Gastroenterology
Pediatric/child health	Hematology and oncology
Psychiatric/mental health	Neurology
Women's health	Occupational health
	Orthopedics
	Pulmonology and Respiratory
	Sports medicine
	Urology

Source: www.aapn.org

WHAT DOES IT TAKE TO BE A NURSE PRACTITIONER?

According to the American Association of Nurse Practitioners (AANP), "NPs undergo rigorous national certification, periodic peer review, clinical outcome evaluations, and adhere to a code for ethical practices. Self-directed continued learning and professional development is also essential to maintaining clinical competency."[1]

Certification

You'll need to be certified by a professional organization, such as the American Academy of Nurse Practitioners, American Nurses Credentialing Center,

American Association of Critical Care Nurses, Pediatric Nursing Certification Board, or the National Certification Corporation. Certification covers at least one patient population focus (such as pediatrics or gerontology). Every five years, you'll get recertified on the basis of seventy-five to one hundred continuing education credits plus one thousand documented clinical hours. (Some certification agencies will substitute a good exam score for the continuing education hours.)

Licensing

Nurse practitioners are licensed by their state's board of nursing. Each state defines what a nurse practitioner can do:

- Twenty-three states use the Full Practice Model: APRNs can practice autonomously when licensed by the state board of nursing. This model is recommended by the National Academy of Medicine and the National Council of State Boards of Nursing.
- Sixteen states use the Reduced Practice Model: APRNs must collaborate with another health provider.
- Two states require Restricted Practice: APRNs can only practice under supervision by another health provider.

Nurse practitioners work with other medical professionals to ensure their patients have the best care. Some duties are the same as for RNs, such as taking patient histories. But APRNs are also trained to order and evaluate test results, diagnose and treat illnesses and injuries, prescribe medication, and refer patients to specialists.

For APRNs, the focus is on patient-centered care, which for many means a holistic approach to preventing illness and maintaining health. In this role, you want to understand the patient's concerns and lifestyle while making a plan for their care.

Many nurse practitioners are also involved in creating new knowledge through research projects. Research supports evidence-based practice, which means practice that has been scientifically proven to work. Other APRNs teach staff or nursing students about new clinical findings, policies, procedures, and the philosophy of advanced nursing practice. And APRNs provide health information to the community through healthcare forums, workshops, and other activities.

Note: According to the AANP, nurse practitioners are more than just healthcare providers; they are mentors, educators, researchers, and administrators. Their involvement in professional organizations and participation in health policy activities at the local, state, national, and international levels helps to advance the role of the nurse practitioner and ensure that professional standards are maintained. *Source:* http://www.aanp.org/

WHAT ARE THE PROS AND CONS OF WORKING AS A NURSE PRACTITIONER?

What one person sees as a pro, someone else may see as a con. Here are some things to remember before you decide to go into the nurse practitioner field.

- You have to start as an RN.
- You need a lot of education—both a bachelor's degree and a master's degree from an accredited program—so you may have some student loans.
- Pay is quite high: It varies from state to state, but an entry-level nurse practitioner could generally expect to earn about $89,000 a year.
- Continuing education: You'll need to continue to take classes, workshops, and seminars from credible, accredited sources to stay certified and licensed.
- Advancement: APRNs can move up the ladder by taking on managerial or administrative roles, teaching in a college or graduate program, or by earning a Doctor of Nursing Practice (DNP) degree.
- Job satisfaction: In general, APRNs are very happy and satisfied in their work. Helping people get and stay healthy is a wonderful thing!

HOW HEALTHY IS THE JOB MARKET FOR NURSE PRACTITIONERS?

The job market for nurse practitioners is very healthy!

- Patients who see a nurse practitioner for primary care generally have lower medication costs, fewer emergency room visits, and shorter hospital stays.
- Patients who visit a nurse practitioner report extremely high levels of satisfaction with their care.
- APRNs help fill the gap in primary practice providers. In 2016, the Bureau of Labor Statistics reported about 150,230 APRNs in the

United States. In 2018, according to the AANP, there are now more than 248,000 APRNs, and they conduct more than 870 million healthcare visits each year.

- The Bureau of Labor Statistics predicts job growth of 31 percent for nurse practitioners, much higher than the national norm of 7 percent for all jobs.
- Experienced APRNs can expect to earn more than $100,000 per year (that's the average—some states pay more, others a little less).
- The nurse practitioner field will continue to grow because of greater emphasis on preventive care as well as the need for healthcare services for the elderly.

AM I RIGHT FOR THE JOB OF NURSE PRACTITIONER?

To be successful as a nurse practitioner, you need some special qualities:

- *Compassion:* APRNs must be caring and sympathetic toward patients. Your patient may be in pain or emotional distress, or may be too young or mentally impaired to be able to tell you what the problem is.
- *Communication:* You'll need to communicate clearly and effectively with patients, families, and other members of the healthcare team.
- *Critical thinking:* You'll need to look at the big picture of your patient's health situation, assess and monitor changes in their health, and quickly decide on what's the best thing to do. You'll also need to decide quickly if you need to consult with another health professional.
- *Detail oriented:* Details are very important—someone's life could depend on just one detail. Because APRNs often provide treatment and medication, it's important to know all the details of your patient's current condition, like what medicines they're already taking, or if something has changed.
- *Resourcefulness:* At every level of your work—as an RN, a college student, a graduate student, and in practice as an APRN—you need to know how and where to quickly find the answers you need.
- *People skills:* You'll be working with patients, families, other healthcare team members, and staff from other labs and hospitals. Always be professional, respectful, caring, willing to listen, and willing to talk so your patient will get the best care possible.

- *Leadership:* Nurse practitioners are often in senior positions. You'll need to lead effectively, sometimes manage other staff members, and teach others important skills and information.

SUMMARY—NURSE PRACTITIONER

Being a nurse practitioner is a satisfying, well-paid career that is also demanding and requires a significant amount of education. As a nurse practitioner, you will improve the lives and health of your patients, educate your community and colleagues, and share in the well-being of the people you help. You can focus on a specific illness or population, learn new things, conduct important research that helps everyone in the field, and be a leader.

A great place to start to learn more about this career is www.aanp.org, the website for the AANP.

Next we'll take a look at the role of the physician assistant. This job has a lot in common with the APRN, but also has its own unique aspects.

Physician Assistant

Physician assistants work directly with patients under a physician's supervision.

WHAT IS A PHYSICIAN ASSISTANT?

A physician assistant (PA) is a licensed healthcare professional who treats patients under the supervision of a physician. There is overlap between what a PA does and what a nurse practitioner does, but there are also important differences in the way they practice. (PAs are sometimes confused with medical assistants, which is more of a clerical job.) Check out the box "What Does a Physician Assistant Do?"

WHAT DOES A PHYSICIAN ASSISTANT DO?

- Provide primary or specialized care to patients
- Work under a supervising physician
- Take medical histories
- Conduct physical exams
- Diagnose and treat illness
- Order and interpret tests
- Develop treatment plans
- Prescribe medication
- Counsel on preventive care
- Perform procedures (including minor surgical procedures)
- Assist in surgery
- Make rounds in hospitals and nursing homes
- Administer immunizations
- Do clinical research

PAs work directly with physicians, surgeons, nurses, and other healthcare professionals. PA jobs are versatile and collaborative. Most PAs work in physicians' offices or in general medical and surgical hospitals. They also work in outpatient care centers, specialty medical practices, and the offices of other health practitioners. According to the Bureau of Labor Statistics, PAs may be the primary care providers at clinics in rural or medically underserved communities where a physician is only present one or two days a week. But the team model is still in place—PAs collaborate with the rest of the healthcare team by phone, etc., as needed and as required by law.

PAs work under the direction of a supervising physician—this is called being a dependent practitioner—as part of the healthcare team, which can also include nurses, phlebotomists, surgeons, and many other healthcare professionals.

There is flexibility in the way that supervision is applied, between practices and between states. According to Andrew J. Rodican,

> PAs work very autonomously in their designated field of practice, although the level of autonomy will vary from practice to practice. Don't expect to follow your supervising physician around by the proverbial "coattails." A physician who knows how to utilize PAs most effectively will expect you to work autonomously within the scope of the practice, carry your own patient load, and utilize your diagnostic and critical thinking skills. In many situations PAs may not even work in the same physical location as their supervising physician, but they must always remain in telephone contact. Typically, PAs meet with their supervising physician at least once per week.[2]

PAs can even own their own practice, as long as there is a supervising physician attached. Sometimes a PA might make house calls or visit patients in nursing homes.

WHAT DOES IT TAKE TO BE A PHYSICIAN ASSISTANT?

Many PAs come to the profession from another healthcare role, such as emergency medical technician (EMT), paramedic, athletic trainer, or medical assistant. PA programs are at the master's level, so you need a bachelor's degree that includes basic science and behavioral science. The programs are generally twenty-four to thirty-two months long, and are followed by nine to fifteen months of supervised clinical rotations.

PAs train in what's known as the medical model, which means the emphasis is on disease pathology. Like a physician, a PA approaches patient care by looking primarily at the anatomy and physiological systems that comprise the human body. PAs are trained as generalists, but have the flexibility to move from one specialty area to another. There are many specialty areas—some pay more than others. Take a look at the sidebar "Physician Assistant Specialty Areas" to get an idea of the options.

PHYSICIAN ASSISTANT SPECIALTY AREAS

Specialties

Acute Medicine

Adolescent Medicine

Anesthesiology

Dermatology

Emergency Medicine

Family Medicine

General Surgery

Gynecology

Hospice and Palliative Medicine

Hospital Medicine

Internal Medicine

Neurology

Obstetrics and Gynecology

Occupational Medicine

Oncology

Pain Management

Pathology

Pediatrics

Physical Medicine

Preventive Medicine

Primary Care

Psychiatry

Radiology

Rheumatology

Trauma/Critical Care

Urgent Care

Urology

Surgical Subspecialties

Cardiothoracic

Colon and Rectal

Gynecologic Oncology

Gynecology and Obstetrics

Neurology

Ophthalmology

Oral and Maxillofacial

Orthopedic

Otorhinolaryngology

Pediatrics

Plastic

Urology

Vascular

Certification

PAs are certified every ten years through the National Commission on Certification of Physician Assistants and must pass the Physician Assistant National Certifying Examination. For recertification, PAs must complete one hundred credit hours and pass an exam.

License

PAs are licensed to practice in all fifty states. State licensing boards have different names in different states. The American Academy of Physician Assistants (AAPA) website has a list of all the state licensing boards.

PHYSICIAN ASSISTANT COMPETENCIES

- Medical knowledge
- Interpersonal and communication skills
- Patient care
- Professionalism
- Practice-based learning and improvement
- Systems-based practice

Source: Competencies for the PA Profession 2012 position paper, approved by the NCCPA, ARC-PA, PAEA, and AAPA

WHAT ARE THE PROS AND CONS OF WORKING AS A PHYSICIAN ASSISTANT?

Some aspects of the PA job are obviously pros:

- PAs report high job satisfaction. (As Rodican points out, PAs perform the same duties as doctors, but can focus more on patient care, since they aren't responsible for budgets, billing, collections, and bureaucracy.)
- You can start from any bachelor's degree—While nurse practitioners must be RNs first, you can enter a PA program with any bachelor's degree, as long as you've had enough science.
- Good salary: The average salary is $98,000; many earn $130,000 or more.

- Flexibility: PA certification means you're trained to work in any specialty area of medicine/surgery. You can change from one to another without further training.
- PAs work shorter, more regular hours than physicians.
- Job prospects for PAs are excellent and growing.
- Advancement: With experience, PAs can earn new responsibilities with higher pay, take on supervisory roles, or gain leadership positions. PAs can also advance by pursuing postgraduate education in a specialty area.

Some aspects of the PA job may be pros or cons depending on your viewpoint:

- You'll work as part of a team, under the supervision of a doctor. You'll have some autonomy, but the physician has the final word.
- Continuing education is essential for all healthcare fields. You'll need to keep learning to stay certified and licensed.

HOW HEALTHY IS THE JOB MARKET FOR PHYSICIAN ASSISTANTS?

So healthy!

- According to the Bureau of Labor Statistics, employment for PAs is projected to grow 37 percent by 2020, much faster than average.
- PAs will be needed more and more as the need for healthcare services grows.
- PAs are trusted as healthcare providers—a 2014 Harris Poll survey noted 91 percent of respondents believe that PAs improve the quality of healthcare. (See aapa.org/media.)
- Entry-level PAs earn at least $66,500 a year.
- Experienced PAs earn more than $100,000 a year, on average.
- PAs help fill the primary care gap—as of 2016, there were more than 106,000 practicing PAs in the United States, and that number continues to grow.

AM I RIGHT FOR THE JOB OF PHYSICIAN ASSISTANT?

A successful PA needs to have some important personal qualities:

- *Communication:* You need to be in close contact with your supervising physician and communicate complex medical issues to patients and other members of the healthcare team.
- *Compassion:* PAs must be caring and sympathetic toward patients. Your patient may be in pain or emotional distress, or may not be able to tell you what the problem is for some reason.
- *Detail oriented:* PAs need to be observant, able to focus on their patient's symptoms and treatments, and know which details must be passed along to the supervising physician.
- *Emotional stability:* You need to stay cool under pressure, especially if you work in surgery or emergency medicine.
- *Problem-solver:* You need to be able to evaluate a patient's symptoms, figure out the problem, and then administer the right treatment. Sometimes you'll need to investigate further to find the answer.

DAVID DICKINSON: PHYSICIAN ASSISTANT

David Dickinson

David Dickinson, PA-C, is a PA in the emergency department at Speare Memorial Hospital and at the Plymouth State University health clinic. He holds a bachelor of science degree from the University of Rhode Island and master's degree in physician assistant studies (MPAS) from the Massachusetts College of Pharmacy and Health Sciences. He is certified through the National Commission on Certification of Physician Assistants. He has been a PA for almost ten years, and has been at his current position for three.

Why did you choose to become a PA?
The proverbial reason—I wanted to help people. Also, it seemed challenging. It's a job that makes you think, there are a lot of puzzles and problem solving.

Biology, chemistry, social science—it brings all sorts of things together. I'm not just fixing a broken bone; I'm fixing the broken bone of an elderly person who's got dementia.

What's a typical day like in your job?

You don't really have a typical day in the ER! I see ten to twenty patients a day, with various injuries from sprains to broken bones, or illnesses, or whatever comes through the door. If they need more care, I'm consulting with doctors and advanced practice staff for follow-ups.

What's the best part of your job?

Working with a team. Working with other care providers to provide the best care possible—the nurses, the doctors, the techs, the whole group.

What's the most challenging part of your job?

The mental wear. In the emergency room, you're not seeing healthy people, the way you would some of the time in a general practice. Everyone is sick or hurt or dying—all day, every shift.

What's the most surprising thing about your job?

How much it's not like TV! [Laughs] My initial interest in medicine was from watching TV—shows like *ER*—but it's just not that dramatic.

Was there something special in your education that helped prepare you for the job?

I started getting interested in medicine as an undergraduate at URI. They have a student-run ambulance service there, and it was recommended that students who were interested in healthcare get their foot in the door that way. I volunteered as an EMT-Basic for a year. Not every college has it, but many do. And if not, you can volunteer with a local fire department or ambulance service.

Do you have any advice for students interested in becoming PAs?

If you want to do procedures and take care of sick people, being a PA is a great way to do that. It's a great way to get into medicine. You get to do a lot of things on your own, but without the time and financial investment of going to medical school. And it's a growing field. There will definitely be more demand for PAs in the future.

＝＝＝＝＝

SUMMARY—PHYSICIAN ASSISTANT

If you're good at science, if you're interested in and capable of graduate-level education, if you're team-oriented and willing to collaborate with a supervising physician and healthcare team, if you're a caring and compassionate person who wants to help people overcome their health issues, then you may want to consider becoming a PA. It's a satisfying, well-paid career with room for flexibility and to make a significant difference in the lives and health of your patients.

To learn more, start with www.aapa.org, the website for the AAPA.

Next, we're going to change gears a little and talk about a career that doesn't deal directly with patient care, but is super important to healthcare delivery: health information technician.

Health Information Technician

WHAT IS A HEALTH INFORMATION TECHNICIAN?

Health information technicians (HITs) make sure that paper and electronic medical records for the hospital or physician's office are complete and accurate. You'll use specialized computer applications to put together and analyze data for patient care and billing, including coding diagnoses and procedures. In this job, you won't be providing direct medical care to patients. You'll be making sure that the care patients receive is properly documented so mistakes are avoided.

Health information technicians make sure health records are correct
and meet state and federal requirements.

WHAT DOES A HEALTH INFORMATION TECHNICIAN DO?

- Learn and use electronic health records (EHR) computer software
- Analyze electronic data
- Review patient records
- Organize and maintain clinical databases and registries
- Track patient outcomes
- Assign clinical codes for insurance reimbursement and data analysis
- Document patients' health information (e.g., medical history, symptoms, examination and test results, treatments, etc.)
- Follow EHR security and privacy practices and maintain confidentiality of patients' records

WHAT DOES IT TAKE TO BE A HEALTH INFORMATION TECHNICIAN?

There are a number of certifications available, depending on how much education you have. This guide will focus mostly on the registered health information technician (RHIT) certification.

Certification

Some employers may allow you to earn certification on the job, but most want to hire someone who is already certified. Certification as an RHIT comes from the American Health Information Management Association (AHIMA). To apply for certification, you need to *either:*

- hold an associate's or bachelor's degree from a health information management (HIM) program that's accredited by the Commission on Accreditation for Health Informatics and Information Management Education (CAHIIM) *or*
- have graduated from a HIM program that's approved by a foreign association that has a reciprocity agreement

An accredited HIM program prepares you to take the comprehensive RHIT exam. In addition, bachelor's degree programs include a management focus that enables you to pursue leadership opportunities, higher salary, or advanced certification. The current passing score for the RHIT exam is three out of four hundred. The exam covers seven domains:

1. Data analysis and management
2. Coding
3. Compliance
4. Information technology
5. Quality
6. Legal
7. Revenue cycle

Recertification is every two years and requires at least twenty continuing education units (CEUs)—more for multiple credentials. AHIMA offers many types of certification. This list is by minimum educational level; each certification has other qualifications that can be found at www.ahima.org.

Some other certifications for people in the Health Information Technology field include:

High school graduate:
- Certified healthcare technology specialist (CHTS)
- Certified coding associate (CCA)

- Certified coding specialist (CCS)
- Certified coding specialist–physician-based (CCS-P)

Associate's degree:
- Certified documentation improvement practitioner (CDIP)
- Certified in healthcare privacy and security (CHPS)

Bachelor's degree:
- Registered health information administrator (RHIA)
- Certified professional in health informatics (CPHI)

Master's degree:
- Certified health data analyst (CHDA)

HIT SPECIALTY AREAS

HITs can specialize in many areas. Two of the most needed are:

Medical Coders (aka Coding Specialists)
- Review patient data for preexisting conditions like diabetes so coding is correct
- Assign codes for diagnoses and procedures to ensure accurate patient care, population health statistics, and billing
- Serve as a liaison between the healthcare side and the financial side of the facility

Cancer Registrars
- Review patient records and pathology reports for accuracy and completeness
- Assign codes relating to the diagnosis and treatment of both cancers and benign tumors
- Follow up annually to track treatment, survival, and recovery
- Analyze information on cancer patients for research
- Maintain databases of cancer patients for the facility, regional, and national use

Most RHITs work in hospitals, some in physician's offices, and a few in professional, scientific, and technical services or in skilled nursing facilities. Some even work from home. Most of the work is done on computers, but you'll also work with paper files. In hospitals or any healthcare facility that's always open, RHITs may work evening or night shifts. The RHIT is part of the larger healthcare team. You'll work with doctors, nurses, and other healthcare providers, but you generally won't work directly with patients.

WHAT ARE THE PROS AND CONS OF WORKING AS A HEALTH INFORMATION TECHNICIAN?

What is a pro and what is a con is up to you. Some things to remember before you choose this career:

- The job outlook is good and growing.
- Salaries are moderate but increase with more education and higher levels of certification.
- You won't work directly with the public, but you will work with other members of the healthcare team.
- EHR systems are becoming the standard, so computer skills are essential.
- You need to be tuned in to details.
- You might be expected to work evenings or weekends, depending on the healthcare facility.
- You'll need to continue your education to keep up with changes in the field and to be recertified.
- There is room for advancement in this field, including management level.

HOW HEALTHY IS THE JOB MARKET FOR HEALTH INFORMATION TECHNICIANS?

The job market for HITs is solid and growing. There is a great need for new people to enter this field and become certified at both the RHIT level (associate's degree) and the RHIA level (bachelor's degree).

- The Bureau of Labor Statistics expects 13 percent growth between 2016 and 2026, especially for RHITs or certified tumor registrars (CTRs).

- Entry-level RHITs can expect to earn at least $25,810. The average salary is about $39,000.
- As the population ages, RHITs will be needed to manage patient data. In addition, EHRs are being used by all kinds of healthcare providers.

AM I RIGHT FOR THE JOB OF HEALTH INFORMATION TECHNICIAN?

Success as an RHIT requires some very important personal characteristics:

- *Technical skills:* You'll be using coding and classification software and EHRs, and keeping up with changes in those systems. Each healthcare setting may use its own system, so you need to know how that one works, and be able to learn a new one if you change facilities.
- *Accuracy:* It's vitally important that health records be correct. One wrong digit in a code could mean a billing error or, worse, a treatment error. It's important to be able to focus on the details and find and correct mistakes.
- *Integrity:* You'll be working with sensitive, confidential information. You'll need a strong sense of ethics, discretion, and respect for patient privacy, as well as an understanding of HIPAA law.
- *Analytical skills:* You'll need to understand the medical records you're working with so that you can code diagnoses and procedures correctly. It's just as important to see the big picture as the detailed one.
- *Communication skills:* You'll need to be able to communicate important information clearly and accurately, both verbally and in writing.
- *Interpersonal skills:* You'll be working with other healthcare and finance professionals, so it's important to treat everyone with the same respect and politeness that you'd like to receive.

SUMMARY—HEALTH INFORMATION TECHNICIAN

HITs are essential to providing quality healthcare in the twenty-first century. In the Information Age, the people who understand how to record, manage, and retrieve information in a meaningful way are key to every aspect of healthcare in every type of setting. With so many certification options, there are lots of roads into this career, and lots of room for advancement once you're in it.

A great place to start is the AHIMA website at www.ahima.org and its "Body of Knowledge" page at bok.ahima.org.

Next, learn about a different kind of technician, one who works with patients: the pharmacy technician.

Pharmacy Technician

WHAT IS A PHARMACY TECHNICIAN?

Pharmacy technicians work under the supervision of a pharmacist to help dispense prescription medication, medical devices, and refer patients to the pharmacist for answers to questions. Pharmacy technicians frequently work directly with the public, in person or on the phone. They also do some administrative

The pharmacy technician is usually the first face you see at the pharmacy window.

tasks like computer entry, reviewing prescription requests with physicians and insurance companies, and inventory medication. Pharmacy technicians work in pharmacies in doctors' offices, hospitals, or stores, independent pharmacies, long-term care facilities, insurance companies, or pharmaceutical companies.

Most pharmacy technicians work in retail pharmacies and drug stores, others work in doctor's offices and hospitals, and a few work for insurance, pharmaceutical, or other companies. Your primary interaction will be with your supervising pharmacist and the other techs in your pharmacy. You'll also interact with customers, physicians, nurse practitioners, PAs, and insurance companies.

While there are fewer pharmacy tech jobs in hospitals, these opportunities pay a bit better. In a hospital, you might be preparing more kinds of medication, such as IV meds; you might make rounds and give medications to patients.

WHAT DOES A PHARMACY TECHNICIAN DO?

- Interacts with patients and customers
- Interacts with physician's offices and insurance companies
- Dispenses prescription medicine and medical devices
- Inventories medication and lets the pharmacist know what needs to be ordered
- Selects, measures, counts, packages, and labels medication
- Operates automatic medication dispensing equipment
- Maintains customer information in the computer
- Arranges for customers to talk to the pharmacist about their questions and concerns
- Accepts payments and processes insurance claims
- In most states, mixes or compounds medications and calls physicians to refill prescriptions

---

WHAT DOES IT TAKE TO BE A PHARMACY TECHNICIAN?

Pharmacy technicians earn certification through an accredited program. This is one of the few healthcare jobs you can get with just a high school diploma or its equivalent (like a GED or a foreign diploma). Pharmacy technician training programs prepare you to take the certification exam. Programs may be at local community college or online, or through the pharmacy company. If you have completed a training program through an employer, it is possible to become a pharmacy technician without certification. However, to keep your options flexible and be sure that you are serving patients as well as possible, certification is best.

Certification

The ExCPT exam is the most common exam for the certified pharmacy technician (CPhT) credential. It's offered by the National Healthcareer Association (NHA) and is valid for two years. The ExCPT exam measures three areas of competence: regulations and technician duties, drugs and drug products, and the dispensing process.

Recertification every two years requires at least twenty hours of continuing education, of which one hour must be pharmacy law and one hour must be patient safety.

Advanced certification is also available. For instance, the National Pharmacy Technician Association (NPTA) offers:

- Sterile products/IV certification
- Chemotherapy certification
- Compounding certification

WHAT'S ON THE CERTIFICATION TEST?

Certification tests measure nine knowledge areas:

1. Pharmacology for technicians
2. Pharmacy law and regulations
3. Sterile and nonsterile compounding
4. Medication safety
5. Pharmacy quality assurance
6. Medication order entry and fill process
7. Pharmacy inventory management
8. Pharmacy billing and reimbursement
9. Pharmacy information systems usage and application

License/Registration

Most states require pharmacy technicians to be licensed by and/or registered with the state. Check with your state's board of pharmacy to find out the rules where you work.

> "It is important for the patient to be able to trust a technician to provide the best care by filling the correct medication and referring the patient to the pharmacist for appropriate counseling."—*Mosby's Pharmacy Technician: Principles and Practice*, 4th ed.[3]

WHAT ARE THE PROS AND CONS OF WORKING AS A PHARMACY TECHNICIAN?

Here are some things to keep in mind about the pharmacy technician career. Which are your pros and which are your cons?

- Pharmacy technicians spend most of the workday on their feet.
- Many pharmacies are open at all hours, so pharmacy technicians may have to work nights or weekends.
- No college degree is required.
- Certification is required and is renewed every two years.
- Continuing education is required for recertification.
- Work is performed under the pharmacist's supervision.
- Job prospects are good and growing.
- Salary is moderate.
- You will interact with many different kinds of people.

HOW HEALTHY IS THE JOB MARKET FOR PHARMACY TECHNICIANS?

There is a healthy job market for pharmacy technicians.

- The Bureau of Labor Statistics projects 12 percent growth in the next ten years, faster than the average for all jobs.
- According to NPTA, pharmacy technician is one of the one hundred fastest-growing jobs in the United States.

- As the demand for prescription medication goes up with an aging population and increase in chronic diseases, so will the need for pharmaceutical services.
- On average, pharmacy technicians make over $30,000 per year. Hospitals pay a bit more, and retail pharmacies a bit less.

AM I RIGHT FOR THE JOB OF PHARMACY TECHNICIAN?

You need to have the right attitude to be successful as a pharmacy technician. You'll need to be solid in these areas:

- *Careful and detail oriented:* It is hugely important not to make mistakes when filling prescriptions. Even though the pharmacist is ultimately responsible, you will need to pay close attention to what you're doing and be accurate.
- *People skills:* You'll be dealing with many kinds of people, so it's important to be helpful, polite, and competent.
- *High ethical standards:* You must have honesty and integrity, uphold the law, and maintain patient confidentiality every day. Find the Code of Ethics for Pharmacy Technicians at www.pharmacytechnician.com/code-of-ethics.
- *Math skills:* You'll need to understand the math concepts associated with counting pills and compounding medications.
- *Technical skills:* You'll need to understand pharmacy technology, such as automated dispensing machines, computer record keeping, and the cash register.
- *Communication skills:* You need to listen carefully and speak clearly to everyone to help avoid mistakes.

SUMMARY—PHARMACY TECHNICIAN

If you are careful and detail oriented, good with people, and have high ethical standards, being a pharmacy technician could be a good job for you. This is one of the few jobs in healthcare that does not require a college degree. There's room for on-the-job training, and with increased education and advanced certification, there is room for advancement, too.

Learn more at the NPTA website at www.pharmacytechnician.org.

Next, we'll learn about another health career open to someone with a high school diploma: phlebotomy.

Phlebotomist

WHAT IS A PHLEBOTOMIST?

A phlebotomist draws blood for laboratory tests, blood donations, transfusions, or research. Phlebotomists work directly with patients, mostly in hospitals and doctors' offices, blood donation centers, medical and diagnostic labs, and other inpatient and outpatient settings. Phlebotomists are trained to be very careful about identifying, labeling, and tracking blood samples. Some phlebotomists also have laboratory duties, such analyzing samples.

Phlebotomists work with patients, physicians, nurses, nurse practitioners, PAs, laboratory personnel, pathologists, scientists, and supervisors. It is important to understand your role as a member of the team, and think about

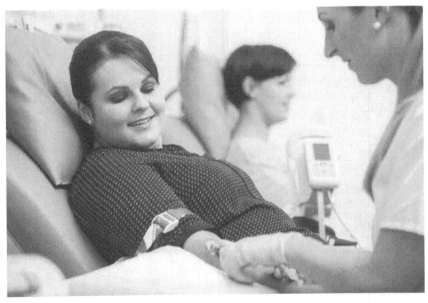

Phlebotomists draw blood for laboratory testing or donation.

what you can do to help the team achieve its goals and provide the best patient care possible.

Some patients (or family members) are fearful, squeamish, or even faint at the sight of blood. Part of your job will be to anticipate issues and help the patients or donors to get through the procedure without harm or problems.

WHAT DO PHLEBOTOMISTS DO?

- Draw blood from patients and blood donors
- Talk to patients to explain procedures and ease fears
- Verify patient/donor identity
- Correctly label the blood sample
- Record patient data in the computer record
- Organize and maintain equipment
- Keep the blood draw area clean
- Maintain patient confidentiality per HIPAA
- Sometimes perform laboratory tests and analyses

WHAT DOES IT TAKE TO BE A PHLEBOTOMIST?

Phlebotomists can train for the field with just a high school diploma or with more education. Sometime, other types of allied healthcare professionals cross-train as phlebotomists. To become a phlebotomist, you must complete a phlebotomy program through a community college, vocational or technical school, or organization like the Red Cross. The program will generally include classroom work, lab work, and learning about anatomy, physiology, and medical terminology. Learning how to identify, label, and track blood samples is essential. These programs usually take about a year and lead to certification.

Certification

Several professional organizations offer professional certification for phlebotomists, including:

- American Medical Technologists (AMT)
- American Society for Clinical Pathology (ASCP)

- National Center for Competency Testing (NCCT)
- National Healthcareer Association (NHA)
- National Phlebotomy Association (NPA)

Certification requirements vary by state. Certification testing usually involves a written exam and demonstrating that you are competent at procedures, such as drawing blood.

License

Only a few states require phlebotomists to be licensed. As a phlebotomist, you may be allowed to perform a procedure in one state that you are not allowed to perform in another.

WHAT ARE THE PROS AND CONS OF WORKING AS A PHLEBOTOMIST?

Depending on what you're looking for in a career, these may be pros or cons for you.

- Job prospects are good and growing.
- No college degree is required.
- Training is short (usually, one year) compared to some other health professions.
- Certification varies from state to state.
- You'll be working directly with patients.
- You'll be working directly with many members of the healthcare team.
- Salaries are moderate.
- Continuing education is necessary for recertification, but also provides increased opportunity and advancement.

HOW HEALTHY IS THE JOB MARKET FOR PHLEBOTOMISTS?

The job market for phlebotomists is very good.

- The Bureau of Labor Statistics expects the field to grow 25 percent in the next 10 years, faster than average.

- Hospitals, blood donor centers, and other healthcare facilities all need phlebotomists.
- Salaries range from $24,250 to $48,030, with an average of $33,670.

AM I RIGHT FOR THE JOB OF PHLEBOTOMIST?

To be a phlebotomist, you need to have certain qualities:

- *Hand-eye coordination:* To draw blood from patient, you need to have steady hands to use the equipment and minimize patient discomfort.
- *Compassion and respect:* Remember that some patients or even donors are afraid or uncomfortable with having their blood drawn. Be caring, kind, and patient. Communicate with your patients and maintain their privacy.
- *Detail oriented:* To draw blood in the right vials, label it correctly, and track where it goes, you have to pay attention to detail. A mistake could mean a misdiagnosis or wrong treatment, and a patient could suffer.
- *Emotional stability:* Every day, you'll encounter patients who are ill, in pain, or afraid. You'll be handling blood and other body fluids. It's important to stay calm, do your job professionally and competently, and be reassuring while you do it.
- *Physical stamina:* You'll be spending a lot of time on your feet, and may be walking all over the hospital to do blood draws.
- *High standards for hygiene and integrity:* It's important to be self-motivated to follow the protocols and procedures, to wash your hands, to report mistakes, and to tell the truth. It's also important to always be learning the newest, best practices for the field of phlebotomy.

SUMMARY—PHLEBOTOMIST

If you are careful and have good dexterity and hand-eye coordination, if you are looking for a career that you can start with a short training period, if you are a people person, and if you have high standards for yourself, you could make a good phlebotomist.

Learn more from the NPA at www.nationalphlebotomy.org.

If you're interested in something even more challenging, check out our next career: surgical technologist.

Surgical Technologist

WHAT IS A SURGICAL TECHNOLOGIST?

Surgical technologists are important members of the surgical team. Under a surgeon's supervision, they prepare and sterilize the operating room before surgery and pass tools to the surgeon during surgery. They manage the sterile field and keep track of the specimens and instruments. This is a position of responsibility that requires expertise in principles of asepsis and sterile technique plus knowledge of anatomy, relevant surgical procedures, and the technology used by the surgeon for both invasive and noninvasive procedures.

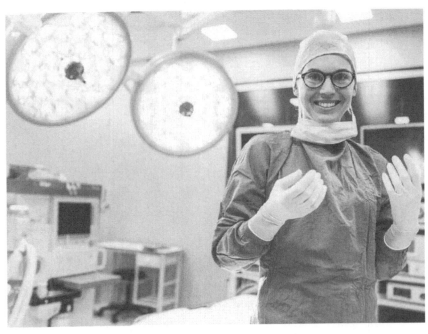

A surgical technologist assists the surgeon during operations.

WHAT DO SURGICAL TECHNOLOGISTS DO?

- Organize and prepare the operating room
- Prepare and maintain the sterile field
- Set up surgical equipment, supplies, and solutions
- Ensure equipment is functioning properly
- Ensure operating room is a safe environment
- Talk with the patient, take vital signs, and help prepare them for surgery
- Transport the patient to and from surgery
- Wash and disinfect patient's skin
- Pass instruments to the surgeon
- Organize, count, and keep track of instruments
- Apply drapes and dressings to the patient
- Hold retractors
- Keep track of specimens for analysis or disposal
- Clean the operating room to prepare it for the next surgery

WHAT DOES IT TAKE TO BE A SURGICAL TECHNOLOGIST?

To become a surgical technologist, you'll need to complete a two-year associate's degree program at a college or through a military or other certificate program. Courses will cover both general medical studies and applied operating room medicine. Then you'll need to pass the National Board of Surgical Technology and Surgical Assisting (NBSTSA) certification exam.

Certification

After completing an accredited program, you must pass the national certified surgical technologist (CST) exam offered by the NBSTSA. Every four years, CSTs renew their certification by earning sixty continuing education credits. You can find the eligibility policy at www.nbstsa.org/policies.

Also called operating room technicians or scrubs, CSTs work with the sterile team to assist the surgeon during operations. Surgical technologists often fill the role of second assistant or second scrub, performing tasks that don't involve cutting or removing tissue.

ADVANCEMENT FOR SURGICAL TECHNOLOGISTS

By building on your training, there is plenty of room for advancement for CSTs. The Association of Surgical Technologists (www.ast.org) has developed the Clinical Ladder program to help CSTs build their skills and their careers:

- Level I: Entry-Level Practitioner
- Level II: Proficient Practitioner
- Level III: Expert Practitioner

With additional education and advanced certification, a CST can move up into the role of surgical first assistant (also called surgical assistant). The surgical first assistant does everything the CST can do, but also needs medical skills for various procedures.

The CST background is also helpful if you want to move into other areas of healthcare. With additional education and certification, a CST could advance to roles like:

- Anesthesia technician
- Central supply manager
- Assistant in obstetrics
- Materials manager
- Medical sales
- Organ and tissue procurement/preservation
- Postsecondary educator
- Registered nurse
- Research assistant
- Office manager
- Surgery scheduler

WHAT ARE THE PROS AND CONS OF WORKING AS A SURGICAL TECHNOLOGIST?

Here are some things to know before becoming a CST. Which are pros to you? And which are cons?

- Lots of opportunity: CSTs are needed in hospitals, ambulatory surgical centers, doctors' offices, and other healthcare facilities.
- Pay is good.

- You'll work with surgeons, physicians, RNs, surgical first assistants, and others on the surgical team.
- You'll interact with patients before and after surgery.
- You'll mostly be working on your feet.
- Some surgeries are emergencies, so you may be on call nights, weekends, or holidays, and you may have to work shifts longer than eight hours.
- You'll wear scrubs, so you won't need a fancy, professional wardrobe.
- There's plenty of room for advancement (see the box "Advancement for Surgical Technologists").

HOW HEALTHY IS THE JOB MARKET FOR SURGICAL TECHNOLOGISTS?

The job market for CSTs is healthy and growing.

- The Bureau of Labor Statistics predicts 12 percent job growth in the next ten years, faster than average.
- As medical technology makes surgery safer, more operations are being performed, leading to greater need for CSTs.
- Salaries are good, between $32,500 and $67,000, with an average of $46,310. When you include pay for overtime or on-call time, CSTs actually average between $50,000 and $60,000.

AM I RIGHT FOR THE JOB OF SURGICAL TECHNOLOGIST?

CSTs need certain personal qualities to do a good job and be successful. These are all very important for the well-being and safety of the patient. You'll need these characteristics:

- *Detail oriented:* You'll be ensuring the surgical environment is sterile and that the surgeon has the right instrument when she needs it. It is essential not to miss anything.
- *Dexterity:* You'll need to be good with your hands, able to pick up various-sized objects quickly, and not drop things.
- *Stamina:* You'll be standing for extended periods of time. Sometimes surgery takes longer than anticipated, so you have to be physically and mentally able to keep going.
- *Integrity:* You must have strong ethics and integrity because this is a very responsible position. You will be entrusted with maintaining sterility in the operating room and protecting patients from infection.

- *Empathy:* You'll be interacting with patients on their way to surgery. They may be concerned, afraid, or in pain. Be patient, kind, and reassuring—treat them the way you'd want to be treated.
- *Stress management:* You'll need to work well under pressure and keep a cool head under stress.

SUMMARY—SURGICAL TECHNOLOGIST

If you would thrive in a very responsible job in a fast-paced environment, are good with your hands, don't mind long hours, work well with others, and care about people, the role of CST could be for you.

Learn more about it at the Association of Surgical Technologists website at www.ast.org.

Next up is a job that's truly visionary: optometrist.

Optometrist

WHAT IS AN OPTOMETRIST?

Optometrists are healthcare professionals who provide vision care to patients. Optometrists hold a Doctor of Optometry (DO) degree, and are licensed by

Optometrist conducting an eye exam on a patient.

the state. DOs do eye exams, vision tests, check for eye abnormalities, and diagnose and treat diseases, injuries, and some disorders of the eye. They prescribe corrective lenses (glasses or contacts) as well as certain medications for eye diseases. They often have their own practice and fit glasses or contacts for patients. According to the American Optometric Association (AOA), more than two-thirds of the primary eye care in the United States is offered by DOs.

Optometrists work directly with patients. They also work with the health-care and office staff, as well as with other healthcare providers. More than 50 percent of all DOs work in optometrist offices; others work in doctors' offices or for the government. Some are self-employed, while others work for small practices or in health/personal care stores.

WHAT DOES AN OPTOMETRIST DO?

Healthcare Activities

- Test patients' vision and analyze the results
- Diagnose sight problems
- Diagnose eye diseases or injuries
- Prescribe corrective lenses, like glasses or contact lenses
- Evaluate patients for other diseases and conditions that need to be referred to another healthcare provider
- Provide therapeutic treatment
- Counsel patients to promote eye health
- Sometimes specialize in one area, such as infants and children

In some states, DOs also:
- Prescribe medication
- Perform minor surgical procedures

Other Activities (for Optometrists with Their Own Practice)

- Maintain finances
- Hire and supervise employees
- Handle inventory and ordering
- Market their business
- Maintain physical location

WHAT DOES IT TAKE TO BE AN OPTOMETRIST?

Becoming an optometrist takes a lot of education.

Degrees

Bachelor's Degree

There is no specific bachelor's degree required for optometrists, but you will need to have taken the courses required by the graduate program you want to attend. That will usually consist of subjects like math, science, psychology, and English.

Doctoral Degree

A DO degree is required from a college of optometry program accredited by the Accreditation Council on Optometric Education (ACOE). This is usually a four-year program.

License

National Exam

All fifty states require optometrists to pass the National Board of Examiners in Optometry (NBEO) exam.

State Requirements

Each state sets its own requirements for licensure. Specific criteria may include continuing education hours, letters of reference, certification, or other qualifications. Licenses must be renewed according to the standards set by the state in which you practice.

Certification

In optometry, certification is voluntary. The purpose of certification in optometry is to demonstrate a commitment to quality. Certification shows that you have more than a basic level of competence. The American Board of Optometry has a board certification exam. See americanboardofoptometry .org/board-certification.

WHICH IS WHICH?

What's the difference between an optometrist, an ophthalmologist, and an optician? That may sound like one of those jokes where three eye-care professionals walk into a bar, but it's actually a very good question:

- **Optometrist:** Holds a Doctor of Optometry (DO) degree and is licensed to perform eye exams and vision tests, to prescribe and dispense corrective lenses, to detect certain eye abnormalities, and to prescribe medicine for some diseases of the eye.
- **Ophthalmologist:** Holds a Medical Doctor (MD) degree and is licensed to diagnose and treat diseases of the eye and perform eye surgery. They may specialize in a particular disorder. They can also prescribe and fit corrective lenses.
- **Optician:** Not doctors—opticians are technicians who design and fit corrective lenses based on a prescription from a DO or MD. They do not do vision tests or write prescriptions.

WHAT ARE THE PROS AND CONS OF WORKING AS AN OPTOMETRIST?

Consider these aspects of being an optometrist and decide which are pros and which are cons for you.

- You're a doctor! Prestige and higher pay!
- But you're not an MD, so there are defined limits to what you can do in your practice; on the other hand, there aren't as many after-hours emergencies.
- Lots of education: You'll really know what you're doing but you'll probably also have some student loans.
- Own your own practice: You can be independent, but you'll also have to handle to business side of things; on the other hand, you can work for someone else if you don't want to own your own practice.
- Opportunity: The job market for optometrists is growing.
- Job satisfaction is high.
- Regular hours and full-time work.

HOW HEALTHY IS THE JOB MARKET FOR OPTOMETRISTS?

The job market for optometrists is very good.

- The Bureau of Labor Statistics expects the field of optometry to grow 18 percent by 2026.
- An aging population means increased vision problems and more need for optometrists.
- Salaries are high: On average, optometrists earn about $110,000 per year.

AM I RIGHT FOR THE JOB OF OPTOMETRIST?

Check out these characteristics of a good optometrist to see if this job is for you:

- *Always learning:* Optometrists need a lot of education to become licensed, and continuing education to stay licensed. Certification helps document all that learning and shows that you're keeping up with the latest developments in the field.
- *Analysis and decision-making skills:* You'll be doing diagnostic tests and exams on patients, figuring out what the results mean, and deciding on treatment.
- *Attention to detail:* Prescriptions need to be accurate, lenses need to be well-fitted, problems need to be noticed before they can be treated.
- *Interpersonal skills:* When you deal directly with the public, you need to be pleasant and put patients at ease, while also showing confidence and competence.
- *Communication skills:* You need to listen to what your patients are telling you about their vision, speak and write clearly to let them know your instructions, and make sure that your prescriptions are clear, too, so they can be filled properly.

SUMMARY—OPTOMETRIST

Optometry is an important job with lots of preparation required and lots of care in practice. If you like to work with people, if you're good at science and communication, if you can handle details, and maybe even want to be your own boss, you may want to become an optometrist.

To learn more, try the AOA at www.aoa.org.

Finally, we'll take a look at a career with a lot of variety and possibilities: sonographer.

Sonographer

WHAT IS A SONOGRAPHER?

A sonographer is a medical professional who uses ultrasound technology to image the body's organs, musculature, tissues, and blood vessels. Sonographers (also called ultrasound technologists or ultrasound technicians) can specialize in different areas that call for different types of training.

Sonographers create specialized images of the body's organs and tissue, known as sonograms or ultrasounds. These are often the first diagnostic imaging tests performed. The ultrasound transducer emits high-frequency sound waves that scan the part of the body being examined, and bounce back as echoes. The ultrasound machine processes and displays the results so that physicians can make diagnoses.

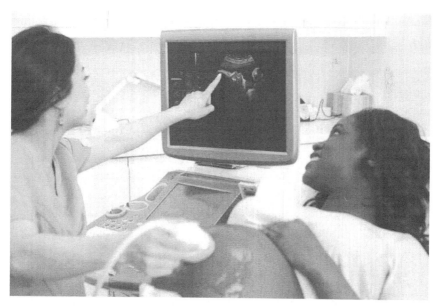

Sonographer uses ultrasound to check on the development of a fetus.

WHAT DOES A SONOGRAPHER DO?

- Prepares and maintains diagnostic imaging equipment
- Works directly with patients
- Takes patient medical history
- Answers questions about the procedure
- Makes sure patient is positioned as comfortably as possible
- Uses ultrasound equipment for diagnostic imaging or tests
- Reviews results for quality and adequate coverage
- Identifies normal and abnormal images and other diagnostic information
- Provides a summary of findings for physicians
- Records findings in the patient record

Most diagnostic medical sonographers work in hospitals; the rest work in physician's offices, medical and diagnostic laboratories, and outpatient care centers. They work directly with patients, as well as the rest of the healthcare team. Sonography involves working in darkened rooms, mostly on your feet, and you may need to lift or turn patients who need help.

WHAT DOES IT TAKE TO BE A SONOGRAPHER?

To become a sonographer, you have some choices. You can earn a certificate, an associate's degree, or a bachelor's degree from an accredited program. If you want to go into cardiac or vascular sonography, you'll need additional education and experience. Naturally, the more education you have, the better your chances for advancement and a higher salary. In high school, it's helpful to study biology, physics, anatomy, and communications.

The Commission on Accreditation of Allied Health Programs (CAAHP) has a list of accredited programs on its website at www.caahep.org.

Certification

The American Registry for Diagnostic Medical Sonography (ARDMS) certifies sonographers in several areas. Each certification has its own exam and relates to specific diagnostic procedures, with their own prerequisites.

- Registered diagnostic medical sonographer (RDMS)
- Registered diagnostic cardiac sonographer (RDCS)

- Registered vascular technologist (RVT)
- Registered musculoskeletal sonographer (RMSKS)

To renew certification, you'll need continuing medical education credits, a self-evaluation survey, and online open-book proficiency exam every six years. You can learn more at www.ardms.org/get-certified.

The Society of Diagnostic Medical Sonographers (SDMS) supports career opportunities for advanced sonographers (also known as ultrasound practitioners, advanced practice sonographers, and clinical sonography specialists). There is also an advanced cardiac sonographer (ACS) credential for those who want to practice echocardiography at an advanced level.

MANY KINDS OF SONOGRAPHERS

Diagnostic medical sonography is used for many different medical issues:

- *Abdominal:* Images the abdominal cavity and nearby organs; might assist with biopsies or other exams
- *Breast:* Confirms cysts or tumors found by a mammogram, the patient, or the physician
- *Cardiac:* Images the heart's chambers, vessels, and valves in an echocardiogram; works closely with physicians before, during, and after heart surgery
- *Musculoskeletal:* Images muscles, tendons, joints, and ligaments; may help the physician find the right place to treat
- *Pediatric:* Imaging of children and infants, often to do with birth defects or premature births; works closely with pediatricians and caregivers
- *Obstetric and Gynecologic:* Images the female reproductive organs to track fertility or a baby's growth and development
- *Vascular:* Images blood vessels to help diagnose blood flow disorders

---

License

Four states currently require sonographers to be licensed: New Hampshire, New Mexico, North Dakota, and Oregon. Other states may add this requirement in the future. According to the ARDMS (American Registry for Diagnostic Medical Sonographers), "Licensure on a state level usually requires candidates to hold a national certification or credential." Be sure to check with your state's Office of Professional Licensure and Certification to see if you require a license in addition to your certification.

Note: "The terms 'sonogram' and 'ultrasound' are often used interchangeably. Ultrasounds are the vibrations and sounds used to create a medical image. Sonograms are the medical image that is created from ultrasounds."—American Institute of Medical Sciences and Education[4]

WHAT ARE THE PROS AND CONS OF WORKING AS A SONOGRAPHER?

Some of these may be pros for you and some may be cons, but be sure to consider the following:

- Pay is very high for the amount of education you need, compared to some other health-related jobs.
- You may have to work evenings, weekends, holidays, and overtime at first, but with experience and seniority, you may be able to work out a schedule that suits you.
- The job market is great.
- There are several educational roads into this field.
- The career ladder is not clearly defined, but there is room for advancement or moving from one kind of sonography to another with the right training.
- You need to pay attention to things like repetitive motions and body position so you don't develop injuries over time—but don't worry: there's a lot of information out there about how to protect yourself.

HOW HEALTHY IS THE JOB MARKET FOR SONOGRAPHERS?

The job market for all kinds of sonographers is very healthy.

- The Bureau of Labor Statistics predicts 17 percent growth by 2026, especially in outpatient clinics.
- Aging baby boomers will need ultrasound to diagnose conditions associated with aging.
- The average salary is more than $71,000.

AM I RIGHT FOR THE JOB OF SONOGRAPHER?

Here are some important personal qualities for success as a sonographer:

- *People skills:* Your patients may be upset or in pain. It's important to stay calm, be respectful and kind, and talk with them about what's going on during the ultrasound process.
- *Hand-eye coordination:* You need steady hands and a good eye to get high-quality images for accurate diagnoses.
- *Strength and stamina:* You may have to physically move or position patients, you'll be standing for long periods, and you may need to work overtime.
- *Technical skills:* You'll be working with various machines and computers, as well as maintaining them to be sure they're working properly.
- *Analytical skills:* While the physician is ultimately responsible for analyzing the images, you'll need to know what you're looking at and what's important, and then document and report your findings.

SUMMARY—SONOGRAPHER

If you like working with people and high-tech equipment, don't mind physical work, and want to keep learning and growing while in a good-paying job, consider one of the many types of sonography careers that are available.

Now that you've reviewed these potential healthcare careers, turn to the next chapter to begin planning your career path!

LATOYA HILSINGER: CARDIAC SONOGRAPHER

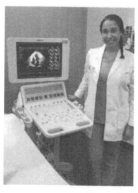

LaToya Hilsinger, RDCS, is a cardiac sonographer in the cardiology department at the University of Rochester. LaToya did her training at Trocaire College in Buffalo, New York. She started her career as an X-ray technician and advanced to cardiac sonographer eleven years ago. She has been with U of R for three years.

LaToya Hilsinger. *Courtesy of LaToya Hilsinger*

What do you do as a cardiac sonographer?
You perform ultrasound exams on the adult heart. You are basically checking people's heart function and evaluating their heart valves and blood flow.

What is a typical day like in your job?

I work in a private office, so it's a little different from what you'd encounter in a hospital setting. We see about eight patients a day, evaluate the patient, do the exams, write up our finding based on what we think of the test, and pass those on to the cardiologist. You need to be a people person, you need to be compassionate, you need to be able to constantly adapt to change, and be willing to learn every day.

What's the best part of your job?

It's always exciting! You never stop learning in this field. There are always advances and new technology. The human heart is so complex—people don't even know! There are so many different aspects to our job, that continuing education is very necessary and very exciting.

What's the most challenging part of your job?

You have to be mentally prepared for the fact that many of the people you see are sick or suffering—especially in a hospital setting, with emergency cases. The heart is so important to the body—when something is wrong with your heart, it can go a lot of different ways.

What's the most surprising thing about your job?

Personally, how much physics is involved! I was not expecting that. [Laughs] There are calculations we have to do for how we operate the machines and what we need for the physicians and the patient. You see this fun machine with all these colors and pictures—but there's *so* much behind it.

Did your education prepare you for the job?

I got my associate's in applied science with a focus on radiologic technology. I went to X-ray school to be a sonographer and chose cardiac as my specialty. You have to do a certain number of clinical hours, working directly with patients, so you're learning how to do your job during that time. I always think that when you're in high school, you should do some sort of shadowing. Hook up with someone who has connections in that field, to see if this is what you think it is and if it's what you want to do.

Is the job what you expected?

Yes, because of the way I did my education. I knew exactly what I was getting involved in. I went out and found a couple of people who would take me under their wing and show me everything. I just had a high school student come shadow me for a whole day. If you're in high school, you should be asking questions about how you can hook up with someone and shadow them. U of R is a teaching hospital, so it's not unusual to spend a day with someone in the field.

Forming a Career Plan

Planning the Plan

Now that you've had an introduction to careers in healthcare, what do you do next? Whether you want to go into one of these careers, something else in healthcare, or something completely different, you'll need to plan ahead. Of course, when you're planning, you need to make lists!

A good place to start is by thinking about your own qualities. What are you like? Where do you feel comfortable and where do you feel uncomfortable? Ask yourself the questions in the box called "All about You" and then think about how your answers match up with a career in healthcare.

Use these simple steps to map your way to your career goals.

ALL ABOUT YOU

Personality Traits
- Are you introverted or extroverted?
- How do you react to stress—do you stay calm when others panic?
- Do you prefer people or technology?
- Are you respectful to others?
- Are you polite?
- How much money do you want to make—just enough or all of it?

Interests
- Are you interested in science?
- Are you interested in helping people?
- Are you interested in moving up a clear career ladder?
- Or would you like to move around from one kind of job to another?

Likes and Dislikes
- Do you like talking to people or do you prefer minimal interaction?
- Can you stand the sight of blood or are you easily disgusted?
- Can you take direction from a boss or teacher, or do you want to decide for yourself how to do things?
- Do you like things to be the same or to change a lot?

Strengths and Challenges
- Are you naturally good at school or do you have to work harder at some subjects?
- Are you physically strong and active or not so much?
- Are you better at math than English?
- Are you better at health than biology?
- What is your best trait (in your opinion)?
- What is your worst trait (in your opinion)?

Once you have a good list about your own interests, strengths, challenges, likes and dislikes, it's time to think about each job's own characteristics. Think about the location of the job—in a hospital? in an office?—and whether that's the kind of place you want to work in. Consider the kind of education, training, and certification you'll need, and balance that against the kind of salary, prestige, etc., that comes with the position. (We'll talk about the cost of education in the next chapter, "Pursuing the Education Path.")

Look through the questions in the box called "About the Job" and see what you think about the different healthcare options themselves.

ABOUT THE JOB

- What kind of work will you be doing?
- What kind of environment will you be in?
- Will you have regular 9–5 hours or evenings, weekends, and overtime?
- Will you be able to live where you want to? Or go where the job is?
- Will you work directly with patients or more behind-the-scenes?
- If you'd be working with patients, what kind of patients?
- How much education will you need?
- What kind of certification will you need?
- Will you need to be licensed with state?
- Is there room for advancement?
- Is there room to change jobs and try different things?

Finally, what does your gut say? Listen to the little voice in the back of your mind that says, "That's the one for me!" or "No way!" Your instincts already know what you'll like and what you'll be good at. A good fit is very important—more important than salary or many other considerations. So think it through with your head—but also listen to your heart.

Where to Go for Help

This section guides you about the lots of different ways you can find out more about the best career fit for you.

START WHERE YOU ARE

If you're in high school, you have a guidance counselor. It's their job to give you guidance about your plans beyond graduation. If you're working on a GED at a community college or someplace similar, there is probably a career office that is there to help you. Take the initiative and walk in the door. Be sure to tell the counselor what you are interested in doing. *Speak up!* Remember, your counselor can't read your mind—tell them what you're thinking so they can give you appropriate advice. And don't stop there!

TALK TO PROFESSIONALS IN THE FIELD

Right now, in your own city or town (or nearby), people are doing all of these jobs. Is it time for your checkup? Start with the people at your own doctor's office or the local hospital. Ask them about their jobs, their hours, how they like it, what advice they have for someone considering the field, and if they can recommend someone else who can tell you more.

Guidance counselor helps a young man figure out his career plan.

Professional Associations

Another great place to find professionals is in the professional association for the field you're interested in. Every profession has a professional association, and there are usually professional associations for subspecialties, as well. This list gives you a few places to start, depending on which field you're interested in. For more, see the resources section in this career guide.

Nurse Practitioner
- American Association of Nurse Practitioners, www.aanp.org
- International Council of Nurse Practitioners, international.aanp.org

Physician Assistant
- American Academy of Physician Assistants (AAPA), www.aapa.org
- American Association of Surgical Physician Assistants (AASPA), www.aaspa.com

Health Information Technologist
- American Health Information Management Association (AHIMA), www.ahima.org
- American Medical Informatics Association (AMIA), www.amia.org

Pharmacy Technician
- American Association of Pharmacy Technicians (AAPT), www.pharmacytechnician.com
- National Pharmacy Technician Association (NPTA), www.pharmacytechnician.org

Phlebotomist
- American Society of Phlebotomy Technicians, Inc. (ASPT), www.aspt.org
- National Association of Phlebotomy Professionals (NAPP), nappusa.org.tripod.com
- National Phlebotomy Association (NPA), www.nationalphlebotomy.org

Surgical Technologist
- Association of Surgical Technologists (AST), www.ast.org

Optometrist
- American Optometric Association (AOA), www.aoa.org
- National Optometric Association (NOA), www.nationaloptometric association.com

Sonographer
- American College of Radiology (ACR), www.acr.org
- American Institute of Ultrasound in Medicine (AIUM), www.aium.org
- Society of Diagnostic Medical Sonography (SDMS), www.sdms.org

JENNIFER MWINGIRA: PHARMACY TECHNICIAN

Jennifer Mwingira. *Courtesy of Jennifer Mwingira*

Jennifer Mwingira is a pharmacy technician at a retail chain pharmacy in a small town. She has been a pharmacy tech for twenty years, eleven of them in her current position.

Why did you choose to become a pharmacy technician?

I was basically invited. I was working at the counter at Osco, and the pharmacist suggested I should come back and work for him. I did my training and certification through Osco's program.

What is a typical day like in your job?

I process and fill prescriptions. Processing means that when a new script comes in, I check the prescription for accuracy and fill in all the data. Then I give it to the pharmacist to check, then scan the label and package the prescription. It's a two-step process. I also deal with checking in the orders, ordering supplies, and talking to insurance companies about issues.

What's the best part of the job?

Nice customers! Being able to help. That, in the first place, was the reason I started doing this—someone comes in who's really sick and they're having trouble with their insurance, and you can go to bat for them and help them.

What's the most challenging part of your job?

Insurance companies—having to call them to override prescriptions and countless audits. They try not to pay and we have to prove that this is what the doctor ordered, and the patient is using that amount per day.

What's the most surprising thing about your job?

The lack of help for mental health patients—it's lacking big time. It's hard for them to get their meds and get them paid for, to get put on the right meds, overprescribing. It's a common problem.

What's next? Where do you see yourself going from here?

I'd like to work in a hospital. It's a different atmosphere and uses a different skill set than retail. It's a little more challenging and there's more variety. Also, it pays better! That's what I would recommend to anyone starting out in the field.

GO TO THE LIBRARY

Skim through some books on healthcare careers and see which one(s) can give you useful information. There are a lot of publications out there. Sometimes you'll just need to look at the introduction, the preface, and the table of contents to tell if you want to look at a book in more depth.

GOOGLE IT!

Do your own research. The internet is an amazing resource. Sure, it's full of memes and nonsense, but if you search carefully, you can find lots of information about every possible career. Try some of these keyword strings to get started:

- So you want a career in healthcare
- Nurse practitioner professional association
- Optometrist business requirements
- State healthcare licensing board
- Physician assistant schools accredited
- Cardiac sonographer certification
- Pharmacy technician jobs

While you're there, take a look at websites for:

- Colleges and universities with healthcare programs.
- Bureau of Labor Statistics: jam-packed with useful, readable information on every kind of job you can think of!
- Job-hunting sites: check out the box "Hunt for a Job before You're Job Hunting."

HUNT FOR A JOB BEFORE YOU'RE JOB HUNTING

When companies want to hire new employees, they list job descriptions on job-hunting websites. These are a fantastic resource for you long before you're ready to actually apply for a job. You can read real job descriptions for real jobs and see what qualifications and experience are needed for the kinds of career you're interested in.

Pay attention to the required qualifications, of course, but also pay attention to the desired qualifications—these are the ones you don't *have* to have, but if you have them, you'll have an edge over other potential applicants.

Here are a few to get you started:

- www.monster.com
- www.indeed.com
- www.ziprecruiter.com
- www.glassdoor.com
- www.simplyhired.com

Making High School Count

As you've seen, different healthcare jobs have different educational requirements. But they all require a high school diploma or a GED. The better you do in school, the more likely you are to be accepted into the program of your choice at a college, university, or certificate program. The more responsible you are now (and the more practice you get being self-motivated, reliable, and conscientious), the more you'll be able to handle a responsible job later—and all healthcare jobs are responsible ones! So study hard and do your best.

This chart gives you an idea of classes you can take in high school that will help you in a healthcare career. Of course, if your school offers any healthcare or medical technology classes, you'll want to be sure to take those!

EDUCATIONAL REQUIREMENTS

If you want to be a . . .	In high school, you should most likely take . . .
Nurse practitioner	English, algebra, geometry, biology, chemistry, social studies, computer skills, health, foreign language (recommended)
Physician assistant	biology, chemistry, geometry, algebra, psychology, sociology, English, literature, computer skills, health
Health information tech	computer science, math, English, science, health
Pharmacy tech	English, physics, biology, chemistry, math, computer skills, health
Phlebotomist	algebra, biology, geometry, chemistry, computer skills, physics, English, health, physical education
Surgical tech	biology, math, English, computer skills, health
Optometrist	algebra, chemistry, calculus, geometry, biology, physics, computer skills, English, health
Sonographer	biology, chemistry, anatomy, physiology, physics, algebra, English, health, physical education

The best time to start scoping out college or certificate programs is in the spring term of your junior year in high school. That will give you time to dig deep, find out what the entrance requirements are, and visit the programs you're most interested in over the summer.

We'll go over that more in the next chapter, "Pursuing the Education Path," where we also talk about the specific education, training, and certification requirements for each healthcare career.

Experience-Related Requirements

Even before you're qualified to work in your chosen healthcare profession, you can begin to develop experience by volunteering, interning, and shadowing current professionals. This will help you build work skills and meet people in the field. Regardless of whether you're earning a paycheck for your work, the payoff in experience and potential recommendations is priceless.

Internships are a great way to get to know the healthcare workplace.

VOLUNTEERING

Volunteering in a healthcare field while you're still in high school can be an invaluable introduction to the world of delivering healthcare. The actual tasks you're likely to do as a volunteer including things like inputting data, charting, and talking with patients. It's a great time for you to get to ask questions and contribute. Volunteering can give you the experience and the confidence to keep pursuing a healthcare career.

So how do you find volunteer opportunities? Easy!

- Talk to your guidance counselor or the adviser in charge of volunteer activities. Many high school courses and clubs require or encourage community service, so it shouldn't be hard to find opportunities to volunteer.
- You can probably find a volunteer role at a hospital, public health organization, or nonprofit organization (like signing up donors for a Red Cross blood drive).
- Try to find something that's genuinely interesting to you, so you'll be motivated to stick with it. That's how you'll learn and how you'll meet people (see "Networking," below).

> "I started getting interested in medicine as an undergraduate at URI. They have a student-run ambulance service there, and it was recommended that students who were interested in healthcare get their foot in the door that way. I volunteered as an EMT-Basic for a year. Not every college has it, but many do. And if not, you can volunteer with a local fire department or ambulance service."—David Dickenson, PA-C

SHADOWING

Job shadowing is following someone around while they do their job so you can see what the job consists of. There are a lot of benefits to doing a day—or even an hour—of job shadowing:

- You get a firsthand look of what it's like to actually do the job you're interested in.

- You see the workplace itself, and what it's like to be in that environment.
- You get some insight into the cultural norms and interpersonal dynamics of that kind of workspace.
- You get the opportunity to ask questions.

Of course, you have to make arrangements to shadow a particular person (you can't just show up and follow them around—how annoying would that be?) But it's not difficult to arrange to shadow someone. You can do it on your own. The easiest way is if you already know someone who does that job. Just get in touch with them and ask if you can shadow them. If it doesn't work for them, they can probably recommend someone else for you to try. Some career centers or college alumni offices have a job-shadowing program you can sign up for.

Dos and Don'ts of Job Shadowing

- Only shadow jobs you're actually interested in doing.
- Be polite and respectful to everyone you meet.
- Dress nicely—if you're not sure what you should wear, ask ahead of time. Keep it professional—no rips and tears, no message T-shirts, nothing revealing.
- Take notes the whole time—there will be a lot of information and you don't know what you might want to refer back to later.
- Ask questions—that's what you're there for. The person you're shadowing is expecting you to ask questions and is ready to answer them, so don't be shy—*speak up!*
- Respect the person's time—someone has taken time out of their day (or their whole day) to show you the ropes. Show that you respect that effort:
  o Ask to shadow well in advance, not the day before; a week ahead should be about right.
  o Be on time—nothing says disrespect like being late.
  o Be helpful—offer to help and do whatever task you're given; it's valuable hands-on experience for you and shows the person you're shadowing that you appreciate their time.

o Stay out of the way—don't jump in to help, especially if the person is working with a patient. Let them know you're willing to help, but don't be underfoot.

- Afterward, send a *handwritten thank-you note*. Sure, you may have been communicating by e-mail or text up to this point, but taking the time to write and mail a thank-you note is so special these days that it will make a great and memorable impression.

> "I always think that when you're in high school, you should do some sort of shadowing. Hook up with someone who has connections in that field, to see if this is what you think it is and if it's what you want to do. I just had a high school student come shadow me for a whole day. [At] a teaching hospital, . . . it's not unusual to spend a day with someone in the field."—LaToya Hilsinger, Cardiac Sonographer, University of Rochester

INTERNING

An internship is a short-term job that provides some hands-on experience in a particular career or field.

- Summer internships may be full-time; during the school year, plan to devote ten to fifteen hours a week to the internship job.
- A few internships are paid but most are unpaid—see the box "Why Work for Free?"
- Internships are a great way to find out if you really like this kind of work—better to find out in high school than after you graduate from college!
- Having an internship in high school can help you get into the college or program of your choice—it shows that you're a motivated learner and willing to work hard.

To find an internship, you'll need to take action sooner rather than later! You may have competition for the internship you want, so the earlier you let people know you're interested, the better chance you have of being chosen:

- Talk to your academic counselor to see if the school has a list of possible internships or leads to find one.
- Talk to people in your community who work in healthcare to see if their employer takes on high school interns.
- Put together a résumé showing what courses you've taken, jobs you've held, volunteer work you've done, and any academic or other honors you've received.
- Contact the place you'd like to work—doctor's office, pharmacy, lab, hospital, nonprofit organization, etc.—and ask if they offer internships for high school students and how you can apply for one. (If they don't, ask about job shadowing programs.)
- If the personal approach doesn't work, try an internet search for "healthcare internships for high school students" near you.

But remember:

- *Do not pay a fee* to any company who claims they will find you an internship if you pay them. You shouldn't have to pay for an unpaid job.
- If you can't afford to take a part-time job or a summer job without getting paid, then taking an unpaid internship may not be a good idea.
- Don't do too many unpaid internships—one or two unpaid internships on your résumé makes you look experienced and industrious, but nine or ten makes you look unemployable. This is not much of an issue while you're in high school, but after you're qualified, you should be paid a fair wage for your work.

WHY WORK FOR FREE?

"Work for free? What? Why should I?" That's a question many high school students ask. But there are actually a lot of benefits to taking a good but unpaid internship.

- *Learning:* Experience is the best teacher. A good internship will give you opportunities to learn about the field that you really can't get any other way.
- *Academic Credit:* In some cases, you can get credit at school for doing an unpaid internship.

- *Relevant Experience:* An internship gives you a chance to work in a field that interests you. It also gives you something relevant to put on your résumé, which can help you get into college or get a paid job down the line.
- *Recommendations:* If you impress your supervisor with your work ethic, you can be rewarded with a positive recommendation for college or for a paid job. Having people in your school and work history who will give you a good recommendation is hugely important as you enter the job market.

Networking

What is networking? It can sound a little intimidating, but it's not all three-piece suits, cocktails, and elevator pitches. Networking is really just getting to know people who are interested in (or employed in) the same field that you're in or want to go into. Recent estimates say that between 70 and 85 percent

Networking means getting to know other people with similar interests at different stages of their careers.

of jobs are found through personal contacts, so it's important to get to know people and, when the time comes, let them know you're seeking a job in their field.

Another advantage of networking is the opportunity to meet mentors. A mentor is an experienced person who gives helpful advice to someone new to the field. Mentors can be teachers, supervisors, colleagues—anyone who knows more than you do, thinks highly enough of you to help you, and has valid advice to give.

So how do you start networking? By being active in the world and looking for opportunities to meet people who do what you'd like to do. For instance:

- *Clubs:* If there is a healthcare-related club at your school, join it and be an active member. Invite people you'd like to learn from to come and speak to the club or give the club a tour of their workplace.
- *Volunteering and Internships:* As we said, these activities give you unique opportunities to learn from and get to know experienced healthcare professionals.
- *Professional Organizations:* Some of these have student chapters or special events that students can attend.
- *Social Media:* Some social media sites, such as LinkedIn, let you connect with professional organizations as well as people in the field. *However,* just as with all social media, be wary of sharing personal information with people you don't know personally, especially while you are a minor.

INTERNAL VERSUS EXTERNAL NETWORKING

Internal Networking

Internal networking means reaching out to people you already know, such as at your internship or at school. These people don't necessarily have to work in healthcare. They may have other advice or ideas that will help you on your journey. Be sure to give back, too. You don't want to be the one who is always asking for help but never giving any! Take care of these relationships. They are valuable in too many ways to list.

External Networking

External network means meeting new people at work, in clubs, in student chapters of professional associations, at conferences or workshops, or anywhere that you don't already spend a lot of time. If you discover someone you'd like to know or ask a question, seek them out and introduce yourself. Be polite and professional. Don't take up too much of their time, at least at first.

Summary

If you don't know where you want to go, how will you get there? Making a plan is the best way to get started on the road to where you want to be. Start by taking inventory of yourself, then consider the qualities of the job. Find ways to get involved—like intern or volunteer jobs—learn the day-to-day by shadowing someone in the career, and reach out to meet the people who can help you on your way.

The next step is to move forward with your education and training. In the next chapter, we'll see what education or training you need for each of these healthcare careers, and how to go about getting the education and *paying for it.*

Get ready to take your first step into the future!

3

Pursuing the Education Path

*I*t's probably become clear from the previous chapters that healthcare is one of the few fields with a great deal of flexibility regarding kinds of work, opportunities in the various jobs, and paths into and through your professional career.

Sometimes in high school, the future can look like a big gray wall of fog, right? But with guides like these, and the inventory of your likes and dislikes that you did in the last chapter, "Forming a Career Plan," plus the section "Making High School Count" in that chapter, you're in a better position than many of your peers to look through that fog and see what's possible for your future.

Education is the key to a great future.

Finding a College That Fits Your Personality

It's easy to get swamped by all the information that's out there about how and why to choose a particular school for college. There's so much to consider!

One aspect of choosing a school that you might not have heard so much about is fit. It's hard to describe what *fit* means, but students know it when they feel it. It's the feeling you get when you visit a campus and it sticks out in your mind beyond the others you've been to. When you hear yourself saying, "This is the one!"—you've found your fit.

But what goes into that feeling of fit? The best way to be sure you can find the right place for you, is to think about what matters to you and narrow down your choices. Ask yourself these questions and write down the answers so you can refer to them when you're checking out schools online and in person. This list is not in any particular order—make a note, as well, of what you would consider your top three most important factors. Some will be more important to you than others, some might not be important to you at all.

Which schools have the program you need? And which feel like the right fit?

SIZE

A school of twenty-five hundred people feels quite different from one of forty thousand people. Each size has its pros and cons. You might prefer the intimacy of a small campus, but find that you don't have enough academic or social options there. You might think you're going to feel lost on a large campus, but find your peers within your department, which might feel like a small school within a big one. It's a good idea to visit schools of different sizes, and tour the department you're interested in as well as the general campus. If you happen to meet a few faculty members or students, so much the better!

LOCATION

There are two primary considerations when you're thinking about the location of your school.

Community

What kind of place do you want to be in? Colleges can be found in small towns, suburbs, small cities, big cities, and in rural areas, too. Where do you feel most comfortable? You'll be there for several years—is it important to you to be able to go hiking or go out to restaurants and concerts? What about travel? Do you want easy access to an airport or train station? Do you want to be able to go to the beach or visit nearby towns and cities?

Distance from Home

If your program can be found in a community college, you may not have to go far at all. Many community college students are commuters—they live at home or on their own and come to the campus for classes and activities. Often, community college students don't need to live in a dorm. At four-year colleges and universities, it's much more common to live in a dorm. But if you choose a school close to home, you could commute to a four-year school also. Or do both—live on campus and go home on the weekends.

So how do you feel? Are you ready to strike out on your own and take on the adventure of living far from home? Or do you want to be able to get home easily, do your laundry, and indulge in Dad's apple pie? Sometimes, students who are the first in their family to go to college find that if they live at home, their parents expect them to continue certain responsibilities, like taking care of younger siblings. That can really eat into your study time. Think about your home situation and whether or not there will be a lot of distractions when you think about living on or off campus. Of course, life on campus comes with its own distractions, so you need to remember that, too.

ACADEMIC ENVIRONMENT

Does the school offer the majors or certificate programs you want? Does it have the right level of degree program? What percentage of classes are taught by professors and what percentage are taught by teaching assistants or adjunct instructors? Does the school offer internships, or help you find internships? Are there study abroad programs associated with your interests? Do they offer everything you want to take, or is it possible to do independent study to fill in the gaps? Be sure to take a look at the box "Your School's Reputation."

Healthcare programs are available right in your community.

FINANCIAL AID OPTIONS

This is something you have to look at carefully—see the "Financial Aid" section. Does the school provide a lot of scholarships, grants, work-study jobs, or other opportunities? How much does the cost of school play a role in your decision?

SUPPORT SERVICES

Support services include things like academic advising, career counseling, health and wellness, residence services, the financial aid office, information technology support, commuter services, and services for students who are disabled, or who have families, or who are lesbian, gay, bisexual, or transgender. Some schools also have religious services, such as a chaplain. Before you choose a school, look through the website and be sure it provides the services you will need.

CLUBS/ACTIVITIES/SOCIAL LIFE

Most colleges have clubs and other social activities on campus, whether the student population is mostly residents or mostly commuters. Look for clubs related to the healthcare field you're interested in, as well as clubs and activities that meet your other interests. There may be concerts, plays, poetry readings, art shows, sports, gaming clubs, and more on your college campus.

SPECIALIZED PROGRAMS

Does the school or program you're looking at have any programs that meet your specialized needs? For instance, some institutions have programs specifically for veterans. Some address learning disabilities. Do they provide mental health counseling services?

HOUSING OPTIONS

What kind of housing options do you want and need? Does the college provide dorms? How many students will share a room? Are there on-campus apartments? Is there help with finding off-campus housing like apartments or rooms for rent?

TRANSPORTATION

If you live off campus, how will you get to school? Is there a bus system—campus or municipal? Is there a ride-share program? Could you ride a bicycle? Will you need to have access to a car? Is there an on-campus shuttle bus services that can get you around quickly if you're attending a large campus?

STUDENT BODY

What's the makeup of the student body? What's the ratio of males to females? Is there enough diversity? Are most of the students residents or commuters? Part time or full time?

YOUR SCHOOL'S REPUTATION

One factor in choosing a college or certificate program is the school's reputation. This reputation is based on the quality of education previous students have had there. If you go to a school with a healthy reputation in your field, it gives potential employers a place to start when they are considering your credentials and qualifications.

Factors vary depending on which schools offer the program you want, so take these with a grain of salt. Some of the factors affecting reputation generally include:

- *Nonprofit or for-profit:* In general, schools that are not-for-profit organizations have higher reputations than for-profit schools.
- *Accreditation:* Most credentialing programs require that the program you complete is accredited. It would be very rare to find an unaccredited college or university with a good reputation.
- *Acceptance rate:* Schools that accept a very high percentage of applicants can have lower reputations than those that accept a lower percentage. That's because a high acceptance rate can indicate that there isn't much competition for those spaces.

- *Alumni:* What have graduates of the program gone on to do? The college's or department's website can give you an idea of what their grads are doing.
- *History:* Schools that have been around a long time tend to be doing something right. They also tend to have good alumni networks, which can help you when you're looking for a job or a mentor.
- *Faculty:* Schools with a high percentage of permanent faculty versus adjunct faculty tend to have higher reputations. Bear in mind that if you're going to a specialized program or certification program through a community or technical college, this might be reversed—these programs are frequently taught by experts who are working in the field.
- *Departments:* A department at one school might have a better reputation than a similar department at a school that's more highly ranked over all. If the department is well known and respected, that could be more important than the reputation of the institution itself.

There are a lot of websites that claim to have the "Top Ten Schools in Sonography" or "Best Twenty-five Pharmacy Technician Programs." It's hard to tell which of those are truly accurate. So where to begin?

U.S. News & World Report is a great place to start to find the right school for you—either campus-based or online schools. For instance, if you're interested in being a nurse practitioner, go to www.usnews.com/best-graduate-schools/top-nursing -schools to find links to the schools ranked as the best that offer nursing master's degree programs.

Determining Your Degree Plan

As we talked about in the first chapter, each career we've looked at has its own educational requirements. Let's take a look at the detailed breakdown here. Then we'll look more closely at each field in the section "Degree Required and Statistical Data."

Minimum Educational Requirements				
HS + Certification	**Associate's**	**Bachelor's**	**Master's**	**Doctorate**
Phlebotomist				
Pharmacy Tech	Pharmacy Tech			
Medical Records & Health Info Tech	Medical Records and Health Info Tech	Medical Records and Health Info Tech	Medical Records and Health Info Tech	
	Sonographer	Sonographer		
	Surgical Technologist			
		NPs must have an RN and a bachelor's degree before entering APRN program.	Nurse Practitioner (APRN)	Nurse Practitioner: Doctor of Nursing Practice (DNP) or a Ph.D.
			Physician's Assistant	
				Optometrist [Doctor of Optometry (OD)]

What's It Going to Cost You?

Costs can be quite different, depending on the field you want to go into and the program you choose. And there are a lot of other factors that affect the cost of your postsecondary education. Are you going to a two-year school or a four-year school? Public or private? How much financial aid are you eligible for in terms of scholarships or grants? How much will you be expected to borrow in student loans?

The following chart is taken from information available on the College Board website (www.collegeboard.org) and represents the state of things in October 2017.

Annual Costs—Undergraduate College/University				
Public				Private (Nonprofit)
2017–2018	Two-Year In-District	Four-Year In-State	Four-Year Out-of-State	Four-Year
Tuition and Fees	$3,570	$9,970	$25,620	$34,740
Room and Board	$8,400	$10,800	$10,800	$12,210
Combined	$11,970	$20,770	$36,420	$46,950
Annual Costs—Graduate School				
	Public		Private (Nonprofit)	
2017–2018	Master's	Doctoral	Master's	Doctoral
Tuition and Fees	$8,670	$10,830	$29,960	$42,920
Room and Board	$10,020	$11,220	$11,170	$13,800
Combined	$18,690	$22,050	$41,130	$56,720

That's a lot of money! *However*, these are averages. In general, tuition and other costs for college tend to go up about 3 percent every year, so take that into consideration when planning for the year that you'll be going to school. You'll need to look closely at the costs of the schools you're considering—they could be quite different from these.

There are all kinds of ways to get those costs down! We'll talk about that more in the section called "Financial Aid, Grants, Scholarships, Loans, Work-Study, etc."

Degree Required and Statistical Data

This section describes the prerequisites, degree requirements, and other important information for all the careers we cover in this book.

NURSE PRACTITIONER (ADVANCED PRACTICE REGISTERED NURSE, APRN)

If you've found the career of nurse practitioner interesting so far, this is the section for you. Here is everything you need to know.

Prerequisites

To be a nurse practitioner, you must first be a registered nurse (RN). You can earn an associate's degree in nursing (AND) or an RN diploma without earning a bachelor's degree. However, if you want to be a nurse practitioner, you'll need to have a bachelor's degree in order to go on to your master's, so it makes sense to start with the bachelor of science in nursing (BSN).

If you already have your RN but not your bachelor's degrees, there are many colleges these days that have programs that allow you to finish a BSN without starting over from the beginning.

Required Degree

Master of Science in Nursing (MSN) or Doctor of Nursing Practice (DNP), plus certification by a professional organization (see chapter 1) and licensing according to state regulations.

How Long Does It Take?

Typically, it takes about two years to earn the MSN degree. It can take three to four years to earn a DNP.

Where Can You Learn More?

Some useful sites to look at if you want to be a nurse practitioner include:

- American Association of Nurse Practitioners (AANP), "Planning Your NP Education," www.aanp.org/education/student-resource-center/planning -your-np-education
- AANP Nurse Practitioner Core Competencies, www.aanp.org/images/ documents/education/npcorecompetencies.pdf
- Bureau of Labor Statistics, Occupational Outlook Handbook: Nurse Anesthetists, Nurse Midwives, and Nurse Practitioners, www.bls.gov/ooh /healthcare/nurse-anesthetists-nurse-midwives-and-nurse-practitioners .htm

PHYSICIAN ASSISTANT

If you've found the career of physician assistant interesting so far, this is the section for you. Everything you need to know.

Prerequisites

Unlike a nurse practitioner, a physician assistant can have a bachelor's degree in any field as long it includes sufficient science courses to satisfy the admissions requirements of your graduate program. Some schools offer a BS in physician assistant studies. Acceptance into an MSPAS program usually requires some previous patient care experience, so it's not unusual for people to enter the physician assistant field after being a nurse, an EMT or paramedic, or in the military.

Required Degree

Master's of science in physician assistant studies (MSPAS), plus certification via the Physician Assistant National Certifying Examination (PANCE) and state licensure.

How Long Does It Take?

Most physician assistant programs take about two years of full-time study.

Where Can You Learn More?

- American Academy of Physician Assistants (AAPA), www.aapa.org
- Physician Assistant Education Association (PAEA), www.paea.org
- National Commission on Certification of Physician Assistants (NCCPA), www.nccpa.net

HEALTH INFORMATION TECHNICIAN

If you've found the career of medical records technologist interesting so far, this is the section for you. Everything you need to know.

Prerequisites

High school diploma or experience in a healthcare setting.

Required Degree

Different amounts of education are required for the different levels of medical records and health information technology certification levels:

High school graduate:
- Certified healthcare technology specialist (CHTS)
- Certified coding associate (CCA)
- Certified coding specialist (CCS)
- Certified coding specialist–physician-based (CCS-P)

Associate's degree:
- Registered health information technician (RHIT)
- Certified documentation improvement practitioner (CDIP)
- Certified in healthcare privacy and security (CHPS)

Bachelor's degree:
- Certified professional in health informatics (CPHI™)

Master's degree:
- Certified health data analyst (CHDA)

How Long Does It Take?

- Post–high school certificate programs generally take one to one-and-a-half years
- Associate's degrees generally take two years of full-time study
- Bachelor's degrees generally take four years of full-time study (or two years following an associate's degree)
- Master's degrees generally take two or three years of full-time study

Where Can You Learn More?

American Health Information Management Association (AHIMA), www.ahima .org

PHLEBOTOMIST

If you've found the career of phlebotomist interesting so far, this is the section for you. Everything you need to know.

Prerequisites

High school diploma or equivalent.

Required Degree

Phlebotomists can begin working in the field with a postsecondary, nondegree award from a phlebotomy program, such as those offered by community, vocational, or technical colleges. Some phlebotomists are already in another healthcare field and learn phlebotomy on the job.

Most employers prefer certified phlebotomists and certain states require certification.

How Long Does It Take?

Expect about a year of classroom, laboratory, and hands-on learning.

Where Can You Learn More?

- American Society of Phlebotomy Technicians (ASPT), www.aspt.org
- National Phlebotomy Association (NPA), www.nationalphlebotomy.org
- National Center for Competency Testing (NCCT), www.ncctinc.com
- National Phlebotomy Continuing Education (NPCE), www.npce.org

SURGICAL TECHNOLOGIST

If you've found the career of surgical technologist interesting so far, this is the section for you. Everything you need to know.

Prerequisites

High school diploma or equivalent.

Required Degree

Associate's degree, diploma, or certificate from an accredited surgical technology program, usually through a community or vocational college. There are about five hundred surgical technologist programs accredited by the Commission on Accreditation of Allied Health Education Programs (CAAHEP). Certification through a professional association is then required.

How Long Does It Take?

Several months to two years, depending on the program.

Where Can You Learn More?

- Association of Surgical Technologists (AST), www.ast.org
- National Board of Surgical Technology and Surgical Assisting (NBSTSA), www.nbstsa.org

PHARMACY TECHNICIAN

If you've found the career of pharmacy technician interesting so far, this is the section for you. Everything you need to know.

Prerequisites

High school diploma or equivalent.

Required Degree

Postsecondary education program in pharmacy technology through an accredited vocational school or community college. Some pharmacy technicians are trained on the job or through the pharmacy company. Some employers and certain states require pharmacy technicians to be certified, and recertified every two years.

How Long Does It Take?

Training can be as little as fifteen weeks or as much as two years (for the associate's degree).

Where Can You Learn More?

- American Association of Pharmacy Technicians (AAPT), www.pharmacy technician.com
- National Pharmacy Technician Association (NPTA), www.pharmacy technician.org

OPTOMETRIST

If you've found the career of optometrist interesting so far, this is the section for you. Everything you need to know.

Prerequisites

At least three years of postsecondary education. Most students entering an optometry program have a bachelor's degree with science, English, and math courses, sometimes with a premed or bio major.

Passing score on the Optometry Admission Test (OAT), which covers science, reading comprehension, physics, and quantitative reasoning.

Required Degree

Doctor of Optometry (OD, sometimes DO) degree, plus state licensure, which requires passing all sections of the National Board of Examiners in Optometry exam. Advanced learning is demonstrated by board certification from the American Board of Optometry.

How Long Does It Take?

OD programs take four years, including classroom learning and supervised clinical practice. If you want to specialize, you'll need to follow the degree with a one-year residency in your chosen area.

Where Can You Learn More?

- American Optometric Association (AOA), www.aoa.org
- National Optometric Association (NOA), www.nationaloptometricasso ciation.com

GABRIELA MILLER: OPTOMETRIST

Gabriela Miller.
*Courtesy of
Gabriela Miller*

Dr. Gabriela Miller is optometrist and president of Montgomery Village Eye Center in Gaithersburg, Maryland. She studied chemistry at Duke University and received her OD degree from Pennsylvania College of Optometry. She is licensed through the state of Maryland.

Why did you choose optometry?

It seemed like a good fit for my personality and my interests. I'm generally a science person; I like to work with people; I like to help people. I worked for someone else when I first got out of school and ended up buying the practice I was at. I like working for myself, and it pays well.

What do you do as an optometrist?

A general eye exam includes checking the patient's vision, the health of the eye in the front and back, the pressure in the eye, and their prescription. I write prescriptions for corrective lenses. I also provide medical treatment for eye injuries or infections. I write prescriptions for antibiotics and remove foreign bodies from the eye.

What is a typical day like?

I run in at 9:00 a.m. (okay, 9:02!) and see patients all morning, every twenty minutes. Sometimes there's a little gap, so I can call back patients who have questions or talk to a doctor about a referral.

What's the best part of your job?

Being an optometrist is really rewarding and really flexible. There are lots of different things you can do with it. I get to help people see better every day. It doesn't get any better than that!

What are the challenges?

The administrative side—hiring, firing.

Did your education prepare you for the job?

I feel my education prepared me for the clinical part of it—what disease is what. But I learned a lot on the job about how to handle people and how to run a business. That part wasn't taught in school!

Is the job what you expected it to be?

Yes—and more. It's more interesting than I expected it to be.

SONOGRAPHER

If you've found the career of sonographer interesting so far, this is the section for you. Everything you need to know.

Prerequisites

High school diploma or equivalent.

Required Degree

Associate's or bachelor's degree in sonography or radiologic technology. Those with healthcare experience and a degree in a related field can sometimes learn on the job and just earn certification.

How Long Does It Take?

- Associate's degrees generally take two years of full-time study
- Bachelor's degrees generally take four years of full-time study
- Post-bachelor's certification usually takes one year.

Financial aid usually starts with filling in the FAFSA.

Where Can You Learn More?

- American Institute of Ultrasound in Medicine (AIUM), www.aium.org
- American Registry for Diagnostic Medical Sonography (ARDMS), www.ardms.org
- Society of Diagnostic Medical Sonography (SDMS), www.sdms.org

Financial Aid

GRANTS, SCHOLARSHIPS, LOANS, WORK-STUDY, ETC.

It is worth your while to put some time and effort into finding out what financial aid you qualify for! Be sure to reach out to the financial aid office at the school you want to attend. They can tell you a lot about what you may be able to work out.

Financial aid can come from many sources. The kind of awards you're eligible for depend on a lot of things, such as:

- Academic performance in high school
- Financial need
- Program/field
- Type of college

NOT ALL FINANCIAL AID IS CREATED EQUAL

Educational institutions tend to define financial aid as any scholarship, grant, loan, or paid employment that assists students to pay their college expenses. Notice that "financial aid" covers both *money you have to pay back* and *money you don't have to pay back*. That's a big difference!

Do Not Have to Be Repaid
Scholarships
Grants
Work-Study

Have to Be Repaid *with Interest*
Federal government loans
Private loans
Institutional loans

Scholarships

Scholarships are financial awards that are usually offered on the basis of academic or creative merit. Some scholarships are awarded for other reasons, such as membership in Scouting or some other organization, or for going into a particular field. Scholarships can also be granted to students who have certain characteristics, such a being athletes, or female, or a member of a minority group. Some scholarships go toward tuition, others are for something specific, like textbooks.

Scholarships are usually given by the college or university, but they can also come through the high school (e.g., a high school might have scholarship money to give to students who are going to community college or enter the field of nursing), or from a service organization or a nonprofit organization. A web search may find scholarship opportunities in your area or based on your interests that aren't widely known.

Scholarships usually pay a portion of tuition—it is very rare to receive a full-tuition scholarship, but it does happen. Scholarships do not have to be paid back.

To learn more about scholarships, check out www.gocollege.com/financial -aid/scholarships/types.

Grants

Grants are similar to scholarships. Most tuition grants are awarded based on financial need, but some are restricted to students in particular sports, academic fields, demographic groups, or with special talents. Grants do not have to be paid back.

Some grants come through federal or state agencies, such as the Pell Grant, SMART Grants, and the Federal Supplemental Education Opportunity Grant (FSEOG). You'll need to fill out the FAFSA form (see "Loans" and visit student aid.ed.gov/types/grants-scholarships to learn more).

Grants can also come from private organizations or from the college or university itself. For instance, some private colleges or universities have enough financial resources that they can "meet 100 percent of proven financial need." That doesn't mean a free ride, but it usually means some grant money to cover the gap between what the financial aid office believes you can afford and the amount covered by scholarships and federal loans (more on federal loans shortly).

Work-Study

The federal work-study program provides money for undergraduate and graduate students to earn money through part-time jobs. Work-study is a need-based program, so you'll need to find out if you are eligible for it. Some students are not eligible at first but become eligible later in their college career. Most jobs are on-campus, some relate to your field but others—like working in the library—could be more general.

Some colleges and universities don't participate in the work-study program, so check with the financial aid office to see if it's available and if you're eligible for it. It's good to apply early to have a better chance of getting the job you want most.

Since work-study is earned money (you do a job and get paid for it), this money does not need to be paid back. To learn more, check out studentaid. ed.gov/sa/types/work-study.

Fellowships

Fellowships are another form of earned money that can be available to students. These are short-term positions in your field. They may focus on research or professional development. Most fellowships provide a stipend that covers some of the costs associated with your education, but are not enough to cover everything.

While graduate students are more frequently granted fellowships than undergraduates are, there are some schools—especially those that are committed to undergraduate research projects—that give fellowships to undergrads.

Loans

There is always a gap between tuition and the amount of money you receive in scholarships and grants. That gap is filled by student loans. Student loans have to be repaid. Interest varies depending on the type of loan. Be sure that you understand how much interest you will be charged, when the interest starts to accumulate, and when you must start paying the loan back. Usually, repayment starts when you graduate or after a six-month grace period. If you continue in school (say, going directly to grad school after getting your bachelor's degree), you can usually apply to defer payment until you're done.

Federal Loans

Federal student loans are issued by the US government. They have lower interest rates and better repayment terms than other loans. You don't need anyone to cosign for your debt. If the loan is subsidized, the federal government pays the interest until you graduate. If it's unsubsidized, interest starts to accrue as soon as you accept the loan. That can amount to a very large difference in how much you pay for your education by the time the loan is paid off.

The most common federal student loan is the low-interest Federal Stafford Loan, which is available to both undergraduate and graduate students. Depending on household income, a student's Stafford loan might be subsidized or unsubsidized. (Note: The federal Perkins loan is no longer available.)

Most schools will require you to fill out the FAFSA when you apply for financial aid. FAFSA stands for Free Application for Federal Student Aid. Note that it doesn't say "free student aid." It says "free application." That means it does not cost anything to apply for federal student aid. You may get "offers" to submit the FAFSA for you for a fee—this is a scam. Don't do it.

Private Loans

Chances are, federal student loans will not completely fill the gap between your tuition bill and any scholarships or grants you receive. Private student loans are issued by a bank or other financial institution. Rates of interest are generally higher than for federal loans, so be careful not to borrow more than you need. Eligibility criteria for private loans are based on your credit (and your cosigner's credit) history.

Don't just take the first loan you find. Do some research, compare interest rates and terms. Is the interest variable or fixed? Is there a cap on the variable interest? Is the company reputable? What are their repayment requirements?

Institutional Loans

Many educational institutions make their own loans, using funds provided by donors such as alumni, corporations, and foundations, as well as from repayments made by prior college loan borrowers. Every college will have its own rules, terms, eligibility, and rates. Interest may be lower than private student loans, and deferment options may be better, as well.

Learn more about all kinds of financial aid through the College Board website at bigfuture.collegeboard.org/pay-for-college.

FINANCIAL AID TIPS

- Some colleges/universities will offer tuition discounts to encourage students to attend—so tuition costs can be lower than they look at first.
- Apply for financial aid during your senior year of high school. The sooner you apply, the better your chances. Check out fafsa.gov to see how to get started.
- Compare offers from different schools—one school may be able to match or improve on another school's financial aid offer.
- Keep your grades up—a high GPA means a lot when it comes to scholarships and grants.
- You have to reapply for financial aid every year, so you'll be filling out that FAFSA form again!
- Look for ways that loans might be deferred or forgiven—service commitment programs are a way to use service to pay back loans. Healthcare workers are in demand for these programs. Learn more at explorehealthcareers.org/secret-to-affordable-health-professions-education.

Making High School Count

While you're still in high school or finishing your GED (or even in middle school!), there are many things you can do now that will help you be ready for college or training when the time comes.

- *Practice your communications skills:* Listening, speaking, and writing. Talk to people of all ages, look them in the eye (but not too much) and pay attention to what they say to you.
- *Build your learning skills:* Take good notes and do your homework on time, but there's more. You also can keep an open mind, ask questions, ask for help when you need it.
- *Make a schedule:* Keep track of your homework, sports, club meetings, volunteering, and everything else you do. Be sure you are meeting your commitments and take pride in doing it.
- *Let your friends, family, teachers, and counselors know that you're thinking of a healthcare career:* Ask them to introduce you to people you could talk to or shadow.

- *Stay clean and stay out of trouble:* Healthcare is responsible work. You might need to pass a criminal records check or a drug test in the future. Remember that your future starts today.
- *Join clubs, play sports, be in a play, or paint a picture:* Try out anything that interests you.
- *Go deeper with the extracurriculars that really mean something to you:* Get involved, show up, invite speakers, and plan events.
- *Take time to sleep and include some unscheduled time in your schedule:* It's good for your brain to let your mind wander sometimes.

Summary

So what's our takeaway for this chapter? Research is your friend! Check out the schools that offer the program you're interested in—first online, then in person. Check out the cost of school and what you can do about it. Keep your grades up, start developing your college and work skills now, get involved—and have some fun!

The next chapter is all about getting the job—writing your résumé, preparing for interviews, doing interviews, and following up after interviews.

Writing Your Résumé and Interviewing

Writing Your Résumé

A résumé is a brief, written list of your educational and professional qualifications and history. You submit your résumé (along with a cover letter) whenever you apply for a job. You may also want to upload your résumé to a few of the many résumé sites available on the Internet. A résumé should be one to two pages long.

A good résumé helps you put your best foot forward.

RÉSUMÉ TIPS FOR HEALTHCARE PROS

- Keep it short—be succinct.
- Keep it honest—don't stretch the truth on your résumé. It's unethical and it could get you fired.
- Keep it professional—leave out personal information like your age, your marital status, your religion, your photo, and your dog's name.
- Format for readability—simple fonts, left-aligned headings, and enough white space that it doesn't look crowded.
- Highlight your education, degrees, and certification.
- Highlight your accomplishments and achievements.
- Include volunteer and interning experience when you're starting out.
- Skip the "Objective" at the top—this belongs in your cover letter.
- Make sure your contact information is correct and up-to-date.
- Check your grammar, spelling, and punctuation—then have a knowledge-able friend check it again.

What kind of résumé is right for you?

TYPES OF RÉSUMÉS

There are three basic formats for a résumé: reverse chronological, functional, and combined. The sample résumés shown here are "just the top"—you can imagine there might be additional jobs, volunteer work, awards and honors, or other credentials farther down.

Reverse Chronological Résumé

This is the most traditional format for a résumé. A reverse chronological résumé is written with the most current information first, going backward to the oldest information last. This type of résumé is acceptable for everyone, whether you're a student, looking for your first job, in the middle of your career, or have great experience and expertise in your career field.

The usual layout for a reverse chronological résumé is pretty simple.

- Name and contact information at the top.
- Education, starting with most recent first (if you've been to college, you don't need to list your high school).
- Qualifications such as certification and/or license.
- Professional experience with job title, dates of employment (month or year is fine), and a short bulleted list of your duties and accomplishments. Be sure to include the things you accomplished or achieved in those roles.
- Awards and honors (if any).
- Internships (if any).
- Volunteer experience (if relevant).

"The chronological style is the most popular with recruiters and hiring managers because it shows a clear time line of your employment. If you have a relatively steady work history and several relevant positions, the chronological format is usually your best choice."—Jeff Butterfield, *Written Communication*, 3rd ed.

Use a reverse chronological résumé when:

- Most of your experience has been in one field
- Your work history demonstrates a clear career path
- You work in a field that doesn't accept functional résumés
- You want to include your résumé in an online jobs database or job search website

---

Russel Q. Nurse, AGACNP
17 Horseback Rd, Boulder, Texas 77777
(123) 456-7890
rqnurse@email.com

Résumé

Education:	2018	MSN	University of South Carolina, Adult Gerontology Acute Care Nurse Practitioner
	2010	BSN	University of Texas—Arlington
	2005	ADN	Navarro College, Corsicana, Texas

Certification: A-GNP certified by ANCC (#9876543210)

License: APRN (License #XXXXX)
Registered Nurse (License #RNXXXXXXX)
DEA Prescribing and Dispensing Authority
ACLS, BCLS current

Experience: Nurse Practitioner   September 2018–Present
Brookside Assisted Living, Houston, Texas
- Provide holistic care to meet specific physical and psycho-social needs of residents.
- Provide person-centered care to those in the dementia unit and the palliative care/hospice unit.

Registered Nurse   August 2010–August 2016
Family Medicine, Corsicana Memorial Hospital, Corsicana, Texas
- Primary care assessment and evaluation
- Patient education
- Assisted physicians with minor procedures

Sample reverse chronological résumé.

Functional Résumé

A functional résumé is designed to highlight your skills and qualifications rather than your work history. Also called a skills résumé, the functional résumé demonstrates that you're a strong candidate for a job, de-emphasizes periods of time when you weren't employed, and helps employers focus on specific skills needed for the job they're hiring for.

In a functional résumé, you break up your résumé information into several categories that describe your skills. The categories should be in the order of most importance to the *prospective employer*. Within each category, you'll include a bulleted list of examples. These should be in order of importance, as well, rather than in date order.

Include a synopsis of your work experience. Even when you are leading with your skills, you still need to tell the interviewer what you've done in the past.

The usual layout for a functional résumé is as follows:

- Name and contact information at the top.
- Summary of your skills and abilities.
- Qualifications such as certification and licensing.
- Awards and honors (if any).
- Relevant skill blocks in order of importance, such as technical skills, business skills, people skills.
- Professional experience with job title, dates of employment (month or year is fine). Include short bulleted items about your duties and accomplishments if the jobs are different from each other in a significant way (otherwise you've already covered this in the skill blocks).
- Education, starting with most recent first (if you've been to college, you don't need to list your high school).
- Internships (if any).
- Volunteer experience (if relevant).

Use a functional résumé when:

- You want to tailor your résumé to a particular job opening
- You have less experience
- You have highly specialized experience
- You have gaps in your employment history
- You have changed jobs frequently or after a short period of time

Carl V. Sanders, CPhT
33 Horseback Rd, Boulder, Texas 77777 • (123) 456-4321
cvsanders@e-mail.com

Résumé

Summary

- Certified Pharmacy Technician with 6 years of experience in both retail and hospital pharmacies. Proactive self-starter with precise and accurate technical skills. Strong communication skills for patient education, customer services, and interacting with pharmacists, physicians, and insurance companies. Bilingual in English and Spanish.

Pharmacy Skills

- Knowledge of safe and accurate preparation, compounding, and counting procedures for prescription medication and sterilized products
- Thorough understanding of labeling and packaging medication according to pharmacy procedure and applicable statutes
- Verifying dosage and refill instructions
- Accurate and efficient documentation
- Inventory and restocking

Administrative Skills

- Medicare and Medicaid procedures
- Insurance billing and resolving insurance issues
- Data entry, charging customers, and balancing registers

Work Experience

- Pharmacy Technician, Rite Aid Pharmacy, Manor St.,
  Waxahachie, TX   2017–present
- Pharmacy Technician, Saint Rhododendron Hospital
  Pharmacy, Boulder, TX   2015–2016
- Clerk, Walgreen's, La Vacance Ave., Waxahachie, TX 2008–2013

Education

- Associate of Applied Science, Pharmacy Technician,
  Navarro College, Waxahachie, TX   2014

Sample functional résumé.

Combined Résumé

A combined résumé is the best of both worlds. It combines aspects of the reverse chronological résumé and the functional résumé. A combined résumé is best for someone who has developed some experience, so that you have something to summarize but you also have an impressive employment history.

Like a functional résumé, the combined résumé begins with a professional summary of your skills and abilities, as well as your achievements, that are specifically relevant to the job opening. Then your education and experience follow in reverse chronological order.

Use a combined résumé when:

- You have a lot of experience and want to focus on your knowledge and accomplishments
- You want to highlight your relevant experience
- You're applying for a job that requires technical skills and expertise
- You want to move into a new field
- You want to demonstrate mastery in your field

The usual layout for a combined résumé is pretty simple.

- Name and contact information at the top.
- Summary of your skills and abilities.
- Qualifications such as certification and licensing.
- Professional experience with job title, dates of employment (month or year is fine). Include short bulleted items about your duties and accomplishments if the jobs are different from each other in a significant way (otherwise you've already covered this in the skill blocks).
- Awards and honors (if any).
- Education, starting with most recent first (if you've been to college, you don't need to list your high school).
- Internships (if any).
- Volunteer experience (if relevant).

Elizabeth R. McQueen
2 Buckingham Street, Boston MA 22222 • 888-888-8888
elizabethr2@e-mail.com

Résumé

Professional Profile
Experienced Health Information Technologist with more than 10 years of experience with increasing responsibility in medical records management and administration. Extensive experience in hospital operations and workflows, staff development and training, policy planning and implementation, and federal and state regulations and statutes.

Credentials
- BS in Health Information Administration, Fisher College, 2015
- RHIA Certification
- RHIT Certification
- Certified by AHIMA in Healthcare Privacy and Security

Skill Highlights
- Health information administration
- Health information technology
- Electronic medical records management

- Team leadership and supervision
- Research and analysis
- Hospital operations

Professional Experience

Health Information Unit Manager   2016–Present
Paul Revere Children's Hospital, Lancaster MA
- Coordinates workload for HIM department
- Supervises and reviews HIM staff
- Led project to centralize medical records
- Worked with HIM Director to develop HIM policies for the hospital
- Verifies accuracy, completeness, and coding for medical records

Health Information Technologist II   2010–2016
Paul Revere Children's Hospital, Lancaster MA
- Maintain security and confidentiality of medical records
- Manage and update patient records
- Ensure accuracy of medical records through interactions with physicians and healthcare providers
- Scan and merge medical records
- Identify and code patient data using standard classification, and resolve discrepancies

Medical Records Clerk   2006–2010

Sample combined résumé.

"Your healthcare résumé must . . . show evidence of healthcare skills, experience and a commitment to quality, as well as an ability to evaluate yourself, your peers, and your department."—Kim Isaacs, Monster résumé expert, www.monster.com

Curriculum Vitae

A curriculum vitae (CV) is different from a résumé. (At least, in the United States—in some countries, like the United Kingdom, the terms are used interchangeably.) A CV is a long document that lists all of your education, achievements, jobs, awards, honors, publications, etc. It is the complete record of your career history. It's a good idea to keep a CV and add to it as you add accomplishments. You might never be asked for a CV, but if a prospective employer does ask for it, you want it to be ready!

The usual format for a CV is reverse chronological order, beginning with your education. Each section contains bulleted lists that relate to different aspects of your career. As with a résumé, do not include personal information. In general, your CV should go in this order:

- Name, address, phone number, e-mail address
- Education
- Dissertation or thesis (if you have an advanced degree)
- Awards and honors (including merit-based scholarships, grants, and fellowships)
- Professional experience
- Published papers and presentations
- Teaching (if different from professional experience)
- Research interests
- Academic service
- Memberships and professional associations
- Languages
- Volunteering (if relevant to your profession)

Writing Your Cover Letter

Your cover letter is the short, personalized letter that you send with your résumé to introduce yourself to a potential employer. A well-written cover letter is a way to show a little of your personality, to highlight where and how your background makes a good fit for the position you want, and to indicate your interest in working for that employer.

You should always try to send your letter (with your résumé) to the person who is responsible for making the hiring decision. Only if you absolutely cannot find out who that person is should you send it to the human resources office.

Your letter should be in business letter format (see the sidebar on "What Does a Business Letter Look Like?")

- Be sure your name and contact information are at the top of the letter, either centered or on the right.
- Address the reader by name—avoid generic greetings like "Dear Manager" or "Dear Director."
- If the reader has a doctorate (MD, DO, PhD, etc.), use Dr. So-and-so. Otherwise, use Ms. or Mr. with the last name. Do not use Miss or Mrs. unless you have been specifically instructed to do so.

A great cover letter can make the difference in getting noticed.

WHAT DOES A BUSINESS LETTER LOOK LIKE?

There are several options for what a business letter can look like. This one is the most business-like, so it's always a good choice.

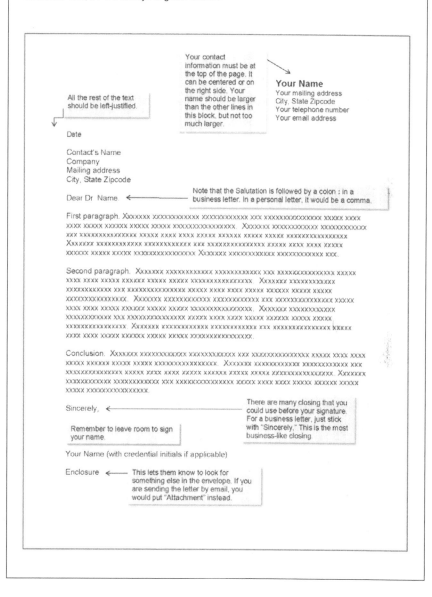

- Identify the specific position you are interested in, and where you heard about it (some companies like to track how applicants heard about the position). Mention that your résumé is included or attached.
- If you heard about the opening from a specific person, mention them by name.
- Highlight your most relevant qualifications: skills that match the ones in the job description and/or skills that could transfer to those in the job description. Focus on your strengths and on what you could bring to the position. Think about this from the employer's position—what about your background will benefit them?
- Avoid negative language—phrase everything in a positive way.
- Your conclusion should include a confident call to action, such as requesting an interview. Don't ask directly for the job, just an interview at this point. Include your phone number here, as well as with your contact information at the top.
- Closing: "Sincerely," (That's it. Don't use any other word.).
- Add a few lines of space for your signature, then type your name, with your credential initials.
- Sign the letter by hand.

FINISHING YOUR APPLICATION

Be sure to follow any and all instructions.

- Write again if you don't get a response within a couple of weeks. Sometimes letters don't reach the right person, even if you have addressed your first letter correctly.
- Following up indicates that you are enthusiastic about this job, and that you're the kind of person who can take initiative.
- However, don't make a pest of yourself. If you've been given a clear "Thanks, but no thanks," move on to the next opportunity.

GETTING TO YES

There is no guarantee that you will be offered the job of your dreams when you first start looking. But here are some tips that will improve your chances of "getting to yes."

- Do your research—find out about the company or practice that you want to apply to.
- Talk to people—especially people you know already or friends of friends.
- Ask about what the potential employer is like to work for.
- Ask about what positions they are or might be hiring for.
- Ask about what they value in their employees.
- Ask about benefits, and the general pros and cons of working there.
- If there is a specific job opening you're qualified for, apply for it!
- If there isn't a specific job opening, send a letter to the head of the department you're interested in, mention your contacts, and ask if they would have a conversation with you about potential openings.
- Be flexible—you might find a good job in a different location than you wanted or doing something slightly different than you originally planned.
- Put your best self forward—everyone you meet is a potential contact for a job (or maybe just a new friend).
- If you get an interview, don't forget that all-important thank-you note! It's one of the most important things you can do to make a good impression. Send the note *that day*, as soon after the interview as possible.
- Don't put all your eggs in one basket—apply for numerous jobs at the same time.

DEALING WITH NO

A wise person once said, "If they didn't hire you, you probably would not have been happy working there anyway." Both employers and employees need to find the right fit. If they didn't think you were the right fit, you most likely wouldn't have thought so after a while, either. Here are some tips to weather the Nos while you're waiting for the Yeses.

- Don't put all your eggs in one basket—apply for numerous jobs at the same time. That way no individual job will become overly important to you.
- It doesn't feel great to be turned down for a job, but try not to take it personally.
- Don't burn your bridges! Don't retaliate with an angry letter or e-mail, or burn the company all over social media. Another opportunity may come up there or with someone they know.
- Keep improving your résumé and your cover letter.
- Keep putting your best self forward—even if you're feeling discouraged, pick up your head and go through your day shining with confidence. Sometimes you have to "fake it 'til you make it."
- Work your contacts—talk to people you know in the field. They may know an employer who would be a great match for you.
- Take advice—if someone (especially at or following an interview) tells you that you need to improve something, *improve it.* This may be an additional credential, it may be something about your interpersonal skills or your spelling or your breath or whatever. If someone tells you something about yourself that you don't like to hear but suspect may be right, don't get mad. Get better.
- Keep doing your research, so if one employer turns you down, you have three more to apply to that day.
- Keep telling yourself that employment is just around the corner. Then make it true!

Note: Until you have the job, every interaction with anyone in the healthcare office should be considered part of the interview.

DENISE SMITH: PHLEBOTOMIST

Denise Smith. *Courtesy of Speare Memorial Hospital*

Denise Smith is a certified phlebotomy technician in the laboratory at a small rural hospital in New England. She did her training at the Jackson Area Career Center in Jackson, Michigan, and then worked for seven years in Nebraska before moving back east to be closer to her family.

What is a typical day in your job?

Busy! I start with inpatient draws at 6:00 a.m. (taking blood samples from patients in the hospital), then come down and open the lab at 7:00 a.m. and start draws on outpatients. During the day, I draw patients, put in their lab orders, and watch the attending list so I know if I need to go upstairs and do more inpatient draws throughout the day.

What's the best part of your job?

Getting to know the people. I'm a people person.

What's the most difficult part of your job?

People who don't have good veins can be challenging. I haven't personally had too many patients faint—in the twelve years I've been doing this, I've only had two people faint. If someone comes in and says, "I'm a fainter," we put them in the chair that leans back and I keep them talking, so they forget about it.

What's the most surprising thing about your job?

[Laughs] People with tattoos all over them who come in and say, "I don't like needles." It's the same thing! It's just a needle!

What's next? Where do you see yourself going from here?

I've been contemplating going back to school to be a medical technician, so I would be doing the tests on urine and blood in the laboratory. It's a two-year program and my boss is really encouraging me to do it.

Did your education prepare you for the job?

I was a nurse's aide for twenty-some-odd years. One of my friends who was a phlebotomist came by the nursing home where I was working. She suggested that I become a phlebotomist, too. I ended up having a ministroke and couldn't lift patients anymore. So I decided to take the phlebotomy course and my friend ended up as my instructor. I was ready, maybe more confident than some of my classmates, but I learned even more once I was hands-on in the job.

Do you have any advice for phlebotomy students today?

Sometimes I see young people coming out of phlebotomy training now who are still nervous and not as confident. They can miss veins they shouldn't be missing. They might be being hurried along through the class where a few more weeks of training would be good. It's good to get a lot of practice and to be confident about what you're doing.

Interviewing Skills

An interview is a business meeting where a prospective employer is checking you out. Don't forget that you are also checking them out. You are both there to see if it would be a good fit for you to work together. No matter how much you want the job, remember that you are not there to beg for charity—you are there to offer your services in your professional role. Be your best self, be confident, and be polite.

To be good at interviewing, here are some things to keep in mind:

- *Be on time*: Don't be late, *ever*. Try to arrive ten to fifteen minutes early so you have time to go into the restroom and check yourself in the mirror before you go into the interview. And don't be too early—that's just awkward.

- *Be polished:* See the following section on how to dress.
- *Bring your résumé:* Yes, they already have it. Bring extra copies just in case. It's helpful and shows that you're the kind of person who is prepared.
- *Smile:* Let them know that you will be a pleasant person to work with.
- *Shake hands well:* A firm handshake marks you as a professional to be taken seriously. Shake hands as you come into the interview, and again before you leave. See the box "How to Shake Hands." ·
- *Ask for a business card:* You may meet with just one person, with a committee, or with several people individually. At the end of the meeting, ask for a business card from each person so that you have good contact information for your thank-you notes.

BE READY TO INTERVIEW

In her article "Before You Interview for a Medical Job" on VeryWellHealth.com, Andrea Clement Santiago offers some great tips:

- Research the potential employer.
- Know the interview process for the position.
- Have solid references ready.
- Plan your route and know where you're going.
- Plan your attire.
- Anticipate job interview questions and rehearse your best answers.
- Prepare to sell your strengths and sell around your weaknesses.
- Prepare a list of intelligent questions for the interviewer.

Read the whole article at www.verywellhealth.com/before-you-interview-for-a-medical-job-1736041.

A GOOD SHAKE

A good handshake will start you off on the right path.

Here are the general rules of handshaking for a job interview:

- The person with more authority (the interviewer) should put out a hand first. If you accidentally go first, don't pull your hand back—that's rude.
- Face the other person, make eye contact, and smile.
- Be fairly still. You don't want to give the impression that you're trying to leave.
- Greet the person and say something pleasant, like, "Pleased to meet you." But don't gush.
- Shake with your right hand unless it's injured—if the other person offers you their left hand, shake it with your right hand.
- A handshake is an up-and-down motion for usually about two or three seconds. Don't pump.
- A handshake should be firm—not limp and not crushing.
- If someone offers you a fist or an elbow to bump, go with it—they may be concerned about germs (not a bad idea in a healthcare environment).

You can't really learn how to shake hands by reading about it or watching a video. Those are good places to start, but you have to feel how it feels. The best way to learn to shake hands well is by asking someone who knows how to show you. How about your high school principal? She didn't get where she is today without knowing how to shake hands!

- *Have good posture:* Sit up straight, make reasonable eye contact (not staring), and keep your shoulders back. Make it look normal, though—like you always sit or stand that way. Good posture conveys energy and enthusiasm for the job.
- *Be prepared:* Read up on the company ahead of time so that you sound knowledgeable during the interview. Here's a great website about how to avoid mistakes at a job interview: LiveCareer.com's "5 Common Interview Mistakes You're Definitely Making (and How to Stop)" at www.livecareer.com/career/advice/interview/interview-mistakes.
- *Be ready to answer questions:* There are certain questions that always get asked at interviews, and there are others that can sound like "gotcha" questions but are actually designed to find out how you handle yourself and what you really think. Check out these websites to get ready for all kinds of interview questions:

  o Monster.com's "5 of the Toughest Health Care Interview Questions—and How to Answer Them," by Catherine Conlan, at www.monster.com/career-advice/article/toughest-health-care-interview-questions
  o Allhealthcare.com's "15 Toughest Interview Questions (and Answers!)" at allhealthcare.monster.com/careers/articles/3483-15-toughest-interview-questions-and-answers
  o LiveCareer.com's "5 Common Healthcare Interview Questions" at www.livecareer.com/career/advice/interview/healthcare-interview

- *Show that you know your stuff:* If you've finished your training and gotten certification or a license, you should be prepared to talk about the field, some of the more recent developments, what aspects of the job are most interesting to you, etc., during the interview.

- *Don't be afraid to ask questions:* Some people don't like to ask questions in an interview because they think it makes them look ignorant. Actually, *not* asking questions makes them look uninterested. Have some questions prepared—both basic and more in depth, because the basic ones might get answered before you have a chance to ask them.

EYE CONTACT—HOW MUCH IS TOO MUCH?

Eye contact can be tricky. Some people get it right naturally, and others never seem to figure it out. Eye contact conveys important social cues. Too little seems disinterested, too much seems aggressive. Either can seem hostile!

So how long is right and how long is too long? Research indicates that about three seconds of eye contact is comfortable for most people.

But then what do you do? If you are speaking, just glance away for a second and then you can make eye contact again. If the other person is speaking, glance at their mouth or away before resuming eye contact.

DRESSING APPROPRIATELY

Business clothes are right for job interviews, even if you'll be wearing scrubs at work.

Since healthcare workers often don't wear business clothes at work, it's easy to get confused about what to wear to a job interview. But the answer is easy—business clothes.

- For men, that means a suit with a button-down shirt and a necktie. Or, if you don't have a suit, nice slacks with a jacket and tie. Wear real shoes—not sneakers.
- For women, a suit is always ideal and is expected for a higher-level position such as a nurse practitioner or an administrative role. If you are applying for a lower-level job, then you could opt for a dress with a jacket, or a nice blouse with either a tailored skirt or dress pants. Wear dress shoes (not sports shoes) but not super-high heels.

Regardless of gender, you should be neatly groomed. Your hands should be clean, especially your fingernails. Your hair should be arranged in a neat and tidy way. Your clothes should be clean, pressed, and well fitting, without spots, rips, or tears. If you wear any jewelry, keep it to a minimum. If you have tattoos, keep them covered. Be sure your shoes are clean and polished.

WHAT EMPLOYERS EXPECT

Of course, employers in every healthcare setting expect you to be qualified and to know what you're doing. (You wouldn't have gotten the interview otherwise.) They expect that you will know how to use the technology associated with your job. They expect that you will take the interview process seriously and be ready with your résumé, your questions, and your answers to their questions.

There are also certain qualities that every healthcare professional should have. During a job interview, potential employers will be assessing you for the following characteristics.

Communication and Social Skills

- Understanding your patient's problems, needs, and values
- Working well with your colleagues in and out of the medical office
- Active listening and clear speaking and writing
- Being polite and friendly, having a good attitude with patients, families, and coworkers, and having a willingness to help

Good Work Ethic

- Working hard at assigned tasks
- Seeking opportunities to help colleagues or employers
- Finding ways to improve processes for yourself and the medical office
- Being on time and not watching the clock
- Showing initiative and solving problems

Adaptability

- Being flexible about new situations, new rules and regulations, new or different environments
- Learning the latest developments in your field and keeping your skills up-to-date
- Getting along with all kinds of people

Enthusiasm for Your Field

- Having a passion for the type of healthcare you practice
- Wanting to provide the best possible healthcare to patients
- Volunteering and/or internships to prepare yourself for a healthcare role
- Having a commitment to continuing education
- Wanting to build on what you learned in school and grow your skills and knowledge on the job

FOLLOWING UP

After the interview, it is *extremely important* to follow up. A thank-you note must be written immediately after the interview. Be sure to mention your interest in the job and one or two things from the interview that interested you most. If you met separately with several people, *send each one of them a separate note*!

Thank-you notes are essential!

Handwritten Letter

A handwritten letter is the gold standard for thank-you notes. (If your handwriting is truly terrible, then type the letter and sign it by hand.) These must be *mailed the same day* as your interview, so be sure you already have stamps and envelopes before you even go to the interview.

E-mail Thank-You Note

An e-mail is less personal than a hand-signed letter on paper, but if the interviewer indicates that they'll be making a decision quickly (like within forty-eight hours), send your thank-you note by e-mail. If you met with a committee, you can make your thank-you e-mail message a general one to the whole committee and copy it to everyone's e-mail address. If you met with several people individually, of course you will thank them the same way.

Just like a handwritten note, start with "Dear Ms. Name" (replacing "Name" with whatever their name is) and signing it "Sincerely," two line breaks, "Your Name." Since you won't be writing your signature, two line breaks are enough.

Summary

There is a strong market out there for all the healthcare professions we've talked about in this book. Line up your recommendations and let people know that you're looking for a new job. With a good, tight résumé and a professional, well-written cover letter, you should have at least one interview lined up very soon! Practice your handshake and your interviewing skills, and walk in the interviewer's door with confidence in yourself and what you've learned. Remember to be flexible about the kind of healthcare setting you're willing to work in and where that healthcare setting is. Keep your résumé and your interviewing skills up-to-date and polished. You may be moving up or moving on at some point, and you'll want to be ready.

Good luck in your career endeavors!

Your future is waiting!

Glossary

abdomen: The part of the body containing the stomach, large and small intestines, liver, gallbladder, pancreas, spleen, and other organs

advancement: Promotion to a higher rank; in healthcare, this can require higher degrees and/or certification as well as experience

allied healthcare professional: Someone in a healthcare role who supports and completes the work of physicians and other specialists

APRN: Advanced practice nurse (nurse practitioner)

associate's degree: An academic degree granted after a two-year course of study, usually from a community or junior college

autonomy: Having the authority to make decisions and the freedom to act in accordance with one's professional knowledge base

bachelor's degree: An academic degree awarded to a person by a college or university after completion of an undergraduate degree program (usually 4 years); also called a baccalaureate degree

bedside manner: How a healthcare worker interacts and communicates with patients; a good bedside manner involves good communication, patience, listening, and kindness

blood draw (or draw): Extraction of blood by a phlebotomist

cardiac: Having to do with the heart

certification: A measure of whether an individual meets professional standards of specialized knowledge, competence, and quality in a particular field; each healthcare field requires its own certification

CEU: Continuing education unit

chronic: A disease or condition that persists over a long period of time

coding: See medical coding

compassion: Sympathetic awareness of someone else's distress along with a desire to alleviate that distress, if possible

compound: Mixing pharmaceutical ingredients to the exact strength and dosage required

continuing education: Education for adults beyond the formal education system, usually short or part-time courses

curriculum vitae (CV): Highly detailed document listing all of your education, achievements, jobs, publications, etc.; can be many pages and is more extensive than a résumé.

degree: A title conferred by a college, university, or professional school on someone who has successfully completed a defined program of study (e.g., AA or AS, BA or BS, MA or MSN, PhD or MD)

dependent practitioner: A healthcare provider who works under the direction of a physician

diagnose: To recognize something (e.g., a disease or syndrome) by the signs and symptoms

doctoral degree: The highest level of academic degree; examples include MD (medical doctor), PhD (doctor of philosophy), DDS (doctor of dental surgery), DNP (doctor of nursing practice), and others

echocardiogram: An ultrasound of the heart producing a visual display to check heart rhythm and blood flow

EHR: Electronic health record

empathy: Being aware of, sensitive to, and able to imagine what it is like to experience the feelings of another person

functional résumé: Skills-based résumé, organized by skills and abilities

graduate: Education following the bachelor's degree level, such as a master's or doctoral degree program

hierarchy: Ranking people (e.g., healthcare workers in a medical office) according to their professional standing; includes direct and indirect reports

HIM: Health information management

HIPAA: Health Insurance Portability and Accountability Act; the law covering privacy standards for patients' medical records and other health information

independent practitioner: A healthcare provider who is solely responsible for decisions, acting on his or her own initiative, without instructions from any other discipline or under the supervision of a physician

judgy: Inclined to make negative judgments about other people

license: Permission granted by competent authority (i.e., the state) to engage in a business or occupation or in an activity otherwise unlawful

master's degree: An academic degree given to a student by a college or university usually after one or two years of additional study following a bachelor's degree; the first level of graduate degree

medical coding: Applying universal medical alphanumeric codes to healthcare diagnoses, procedures, medical services, and equipment

musculoskeletal: The body system made up of muscles, bones, ligaments, and tendons

nurse practitioner: Advanced practice nurse; holds at least a master's degree with advanced training

obstetrics-gynecology (OB/GYN): The branch of medicine dealing with the female reproductive system, including all stages of pregnancy

optometrist: Healthcare professional with a Doctor of Optometry degree who is licensed by the state to conduct eye exams, vision tests, check for eye abnormalities, and diagnose and treat diseases, injuries, and some disorders of the eye

PA: Physician assistant

patient: (1) Someone awaiting or receiving medical care; (2) accepting or tolerating delay, trouble, or suffering without complaining

pediatric: The branch of medicine treating infants and children

pharmacist: Healthcare professional who is qualified to prepare and dispense medicinal drugs

pharmacy technologist: Healthcare professional who works under the supervision of a pharmacist to help dispense prescription medication and medical devices

phlebotomist: Healthcare professional who draws blood for testing or donation

physician assistant: Licensed healthcare professional who treats patients under the supervision of a physician

postgraduate: After the completion of an advanced (graduate) degree

postsecondary: After high school or GED

prescribe: To recommend and authorize the use of a medication or drug as a treatment for someone, particularly in writing

RHIT: Registered health information technician

registered nurse: Healthcare professional who has graduated from a college's nursing program or from a school of nursing and has passed a national licensing exam

résumé: A brief written account of personal, educational, and professional qualifications and experience, as that prepared by an applicant for a job

reverse chronological résumé: Written with the most current information first, going backward to the oldest information last

RN: Registered nurse

skills-based résumé: Functional résumé, organized by skills and abilities

sonographer: A medical professional who uses ultrasound technology

sonography: Analysis of an ultrasound resulting in a graphical representation of its component frequencies

specs: Specifications, details, or requirements

stress: Mental or emotional strain resulting from demanding or adverse circumstances

succinct: Expressed briefly and clearly

surgical technologist: Medical professional who assists with surgery; second scrub

ultrasound: Sound or other vibrations having an ultrasonic frequency; an ultrasound scan, sonogram

undergraduate: Associate's or bachelor's degree level

vascular: Having to do with blood vessels

Notes

Chapter 1

1. American Association of Nurse Practitioners, "What's an NP?" www.aanp.org/all-about-nps/what-is-an-np.

2. Andrew J. Rodican, *The Ultimate Guide to Getting into Physician Assistant School*, 4th ed. (New York: McGraw Hill Education, 2017).

3. *Mosby's Pharmacy Technician: Principles and Practice*, 4th ed. (St. Louis: Elsevier, 2016).

4. American Institute of Medical Sciences and Education, "Which Is Better: Medical Sonography Certificate or Degree?" November 9, 2017.

Further Resources

Resources for Nurse Practitioners

Advanced Practitioner Society for Hematology and Oncology
www.apsho.org
For advanced practitioners in oncology: nurse practitioners, physician assistants, clinical nurse specialists, advanced degree nurses, and pharmacists.

American Academy of Emergency Nurse Practitioners
aaenp-natl.org
Professional association for nurse practitioners who provide emergency care for patients of all ages and acuities in collaboration with an interdisciplinary team.

American Association of Nurse Practitioners (AANP)
www.aanp.org
AANP is the main national professional membership organization for NPs of all specialties.

American Nurses Credentialing Center
www.nursingworld.org/our-certifications
Provides numerous certifications for nurse practitioners in different specialty areas.

Doctors of Nursing Practice
www.doctorsofnursingpractice.org
Provides information and advocacy for those interested in being advanced practice nurses at the doctoral level.

Gerontological Advanced Practice Nurses Association
www.gapna.org
Continuing education conferences and advocacy to meet the needs of advanced practice nurses providing care for older adults.

International Council of Nurse Practitioners
international.aanp.org
An international resource for nurses, nurse practitioners, and advanced practice nurses.

Nancy Brook, *The Nurse Practitioner's Bag: Become a Healer, Make a Difference, and Create the Career of Your Dreams* (Stanford, CA: Difference Press, 2015).

Resources for Physician Assistants

American Academy of Physician Assistants (AAPA)
www.aapa.org
The national professional society for physician assistants. The site maintains two important lists:

- State Licensing Boards for Physician Assistants: www.aapa.org/advocacy -central/state-advocacy/state-licensing/list-of-licensing-boards
- Specialty Organizations for Physician Assistants: www.aapa.org/about/ constituent-organizations/specialty-organizations

American Association of Surgical Physician Assistants (AASPA)
www.aaspa.com
AASPA is the leading support organization representing all PAs who manage surgical patients.

Physician Assistant (PA-C) Academic and Career Information
web.csulb.edu/colleges/cnsm/sas/hpao/docs/physician-assistant-2017.pdf
Flyer from the Health Professions Advising Office at California State University– Long Beach.

National Commission on Certification of Physician Assistants (NCCPA)
www.nccpa.net
"The only certifying organization for physician assistants in the United States."

Jessi Rodriguez Ohanesian, *The Ultimate Guide to the Physician Assistant Professions* (New York: McGraw Hill Education, 2014).

Resources for Health Information Technologists

American Health Information Management Association (AHIMA)
www.ahima.org
Premier association of health information management (HIM) professionals worldwide. Offers many levels of HIM certification.

American Medical Informatics Association (AMIA)
www.amia.org
"AMIA aims to lead the way in transforming health care through trusted science, education, and the practice of informatics."

Certification Commission for Health Information Technology
www.cchit.org   ·
Offers government-regulated certifications and its own certification program.

Health Information and Management Systems Society (HIMSS)
www.himss.org
Organization advocating to optimize healthcare outcomes through information and technology.

Pamela K. Oachs and Amy Watters, *Health Information Management: Concepts, Principles, and Practice* (Chicago: American Health Information Management Association, 2016).

Resources for Optometrists

American Optometric Association (AOA)
www.aoa.org
"The leading authority on quality care and an advocate for our nation's health, representing more than 44,000 doctors of optometry (O.D.), optometric professionals and optometry students."

National Optometric Association (NOA)
www.nationaloptometricassociation.com
A nonprofit organization to encourage minorities to enter the field of optometry.

World Council of Optometry (WCO)
worldcouncilofoptometry.info
Promotes improved access to vision care through education and awareness campaigns.

Alan H. Cleinman, *A Different Perspective: An Entrepreneur's Observations on Optometry, Business, and Life* (Oneonta, NY: Cleinman Performance Partners, 2015).

Resources for Pharmacy Technicians

American Association of Pharmacy Technicians (AAPT)
www.pharmacytechnician.com
Provides leadership, networking, and continuing education for pharmacy technicians. Includes the AAPT Pharmacy Technician Code of Ethics at https://www.pharmacytechnician.com/code-of-ethics/

Pharmacy Technician Educators Council
www.pharmacytecheducators.com
"Unites, supports, and empowers educators in the education and training of pharmacy technicians."

National Pharmacy Technician Association (NPTA)
www.pharmacytechnician.org
"The world's largest professional organization established specifically for pharmacy technicians. The association is dedicated to advancing the value of pharmacy technicians and the vital roles they play in pharmaceutical care."

- Online training
- Certificate programs in sterile products, chemotherapy, and compounding

Jennifer Janson, *Mosby's Pharmacy Technician: Principles and Practice*, 4th ed. (St. Louis, MO: Elsevier, 2016).

Resources for Phlebotomists

American Society of Phlebotomy Technicians, Inc. (ASPT)
www.aspt.org
Professional association for phlebotomists. Offers certification and certification verification.

National Association of Phlebotomy Professionals (NAPP)
nappusa.org.tripod.com
"An education and advocacy group for all medical professionals who practice phlebotomy."

National Phlebotomy Association (NPA)
www.nationalphlebotomy.org
Nonprofit organization for phlebotomist education and certification.

Diana Garza and Kathleen Becan-McBride, *Phlebotomy Handbook*, 9th ed. (Upper Saddle River, NJ: Pearson, 2015).

Resources for Sonographers

American College of Radiology (ACR)
www.acr.org
Professional organization for radiologists, radiation oncologists, nuclear medicine physicians and medical physicists.

American Institute of Ultrasound in Medicine (AIUM)
www.aium.org
A multidisciplinary medical association for physicians, sonographers, scientists, students, and other health care providers to advance the safe and effective use of ultrasound in medicine.

American Registry for Diagnostic Medical Sonography (ARDMS)
www.ardms.org
Administers examinations and awards credentials. Offers certification in numerous types of sonography and ultrasound.

American Society of Echocardiography (ASE)
asecho.org
Professional organization for physicians, cardiovascular sonographers, nurses and scientists involved in echocardiography, the use of ultrasound to image the heart and cardiovascular system.

American Society of Radiologic Technologists
www.asrt.org
Professional association for the medical imaging and radiation therapy community.

Cardiovascular Credentialing International (CCI)
www.cci-online.org
Independent not-for-profit corporation that administers credentialing examinations for Cardiovascular Technology and emerging medical professionals.

International Society of Radiographers and Radiological Technologists
www.isrrt.org

"ISRRT is the only organization representing all disciplines of Medical Radiation Technologists internationally."

Steven M. Penny, *Introduction to Sonography and Patient Care* (Philadelphia: Wolters Kluwer, 2016).

Resources for Surgical Technologists

Accreditation Review Council on Education in Surgical Technology
www.arcst.org
Private, nonprofit accreditation services agency providing national recognition for higher education programs in surgical technology and surgical assisting.

Association of Surgical Assistants (ASA)
www.surgicalassistant.org
Professional association for surgical assistants.

Association of Surgical Technologists (AST)
www.ast.org
Professional organization for surgical technologists.

National Board of Surgical Technology and Surgical Assisting (NBSTSA)
www.nbstsa.org
Provides professional certification of surgical technologists (CST) and surgical first assistants (CSFA).

Joanna Kotcher Fuller, *Surgical Technology: Principles and Practice*, 7th ed. (St. Louis: Elsevier, 2018).

Other Useful Resources

Association for Healthcare Volunteer Resource Professionals (AHVRP)
www.ahvrp.org
Premier membership society for healthcare volunteer services

BigFutureTM: Health and Medicine Majors: The Basics
bigfuture.collegeboard.org/explore-careers/college-majors/health-and-medicine
-majors-the-basics
Quick outline of lots of healthcare professions with links to even more—from
the College Board (the SAT people).

Bureau of Labor Statistics, US Department of Labor, Healthcare Occupations
www.bls.gov/ooh/healthcare
Useful and interesting statistics about almost every job or career available in the
United States, presented in a well-organized and easy to understand way. This
link goes to jobs in the healthcare field.

Commission on Accreditation of Allied Health Education Programs (CAAHEP)
www.caahep.org
Accredits postsecondary programs in health science professions.

Christine Sarickas, "Complete Guide to Internships for High School Students,"
PrepScholar, blog.prepscholar.com/internships-for-high-school-students

Explore Health Careers
explorehealthcareers.org
Addresses the underrepresentation of minorities in the workforce and the
shortage of health professionals in medically underserved communities.
Provides extensive information about:

- Types of health careers
- Health career searches
- Paying for college
- Education
- Events
- Other resources

Campus Explorer, "How Does a College Get Its Reputation?" www.campus
explorer.com/college-advice-tips/886F7520/How-Does-A-College-Get-Its
-Reputation

Sarah Brandenberger, "Job Shadowing: The Dos and Don'ts," Maps & Genes, February 2, 2016, mapsandgenes.wordpress.com/2016/02/02/job-sha dowing-the-dos-and-donts

National Healthcare Association (NHA)
www.nhanow.com
Provides certification for those working in the allied health fields, such as:

- Medical assistant (CCMA)
- Phlebotomy technician (CPT)
- Medical administrative assistant (CMAA)
- EKG technician (CET)
- Electronic health records specialist (CEHRS)
- Pharmacy technician (CPhT)
- Billing and coding specialist (CBCS)
- Patient care technician (CPCT/A)

Kim Isaacs, "Résumé Tips for Healthcare Professionals," Monster.com, www .monster.com/career-advice/article/healthcare-resume-tips

Bibliography

Aitchison, Steven, "6 Ways to Dramatically Improve Your Eye Contact Skills." *Change Your Thoughts, Change Your Life.* Retrieved July 19, 2018, from www.stevenaitchison.co.uk/6-ways-to-dramatically-improve-your-eye-contact-skills.

AllHealthCare.com, "15 Toughest Interview Questions (and Answers!)." Retrieved July 19, 2018, from allhealthcare.monster.com/careers/articles/3483-15-toughest-interview-questions-and-answers

American Academy of Ophthalmology. "Difference between an Ophthalmologist, Optometrist and Optician." American Association for Pediatric Ophthalmology and Strabismus. Retrieved July 10, 2018, from aapos.org/terms/show/132.

American Institute of Medical Sciences and Education. "Which Is Better: Medical Sonography Certificate or Degree?" November 9, 2017. Retrived July 9, 2018, from www.aimseducation.edu/blog/medical-sonography-certificate-vs-degree.

Aspiring Docs (pseudonym). "Finding Healthcare-Related Volunteer Opportunities." AAMC: Association of American Medical Colleges. Retrieved July 9, 2018, from students-residents.aamc.org/applying-medical-school/article/finding-health-care-related-volunteer-opportunitie.

Brandenberger, Sarah. "Job Shadowing: The Dos and Don'ts." Maps & Genes, February 2, 2016. Retrieved July 12, 2018, mapsandgenes.wordpress.com/2016/02/02/job-shadowing-the-dos-and-donts.

Brook, Nancy. *The Nurse Practioner's Bag: Become a Healer, Make a Difference, and Create the Career of Your Dreams.* Stanford, CA: Difference Press, 2015.

Bureau of Labor Statistics, US Department of Labor, Healthcare Occupations. www.bls.gov/ooh/healthcare.

Butterfield, Jeff. *Written Communication*, 3rd ed. Boston: Cengage, 2017.

Campus Explorer. "How Does a College Get Its Reputation?" Retrieved July 13, 2018, from www.campusexplorer.com/college-advice-tips/886F7520/How-Does-A-College-Get-Its-Reputation.

Chaplan, Brooke. "6 Networking Tips for Navigating a Career in Healthcare." Health eCareers, October 20, 2017. Retrieved July 16, 2018, www.healthe careers.com/article/career/6-networking-tips-for-navigating-a-career-in -healthcare.

Conlan, Catherine. "5 of the Toughest Health Care Interview Questions—and How to Answer Them." Retrieved July 9, 2018, from www.monster.com/ career-advice/article/toughest-health-care-interview-questions.

Dowd, Mary. "Pros & Cons of Being an Ultrasound Technician" *Chron*, last updated June 26, 2018. Retrieved July 9, 2018, work.chron.com/ pros-cons-being-ultrasound-technician-31135.html.

Explore Health Careers. "Paying for College." Retrieved July 13, 2018, from explorehealthcareers.org/your-education/paying-for-college.

Farnen, Karen. "Career Advice: Surgical Assistant vs. Surgical Technologist." The Nest, 2016. Retrieved July 9, 2018, woman.thenest.com/surgical -assistant-vs-surgical-technologist-22768.html.

Fuller, Joanna Kotcher. *Surgical Technology: Principles and Practice*, 7th ed. St. Louis: Elsevier, 2018.

Garza, Diana, and Kathleen Becan-McBride. *Phlebotomy Handbook*, 9th ed. Upper Saddle River, NJ: Pearson, 2015.

Go College. "Types of Scholarships." Retrieved July 13, 2018, from www.go college.com/financial-aid/scholarships/types.

GrooveJob.com. "Dos and Don'ts for Job Shadowing." Retrieved July 12, 2018, www.groovejob.com/resources/teen-job-resources/dos-and-donts-for-job -shadowing.html.

Harris School of Business. "What's the Difference between a Surgical Technologist and a Surgical Assistant?" Retrieved July 9, 2018, from www .harrisschool.edu/what-is-the-difference-between-a-surgical-technologist -and-a-surgical-assistant.

Isaacs, Kim. "Resume Tips for Healthcare Professionals." Retrieved July 13, 2018, from www.monster.com/career-advice/article/healthcare-resume-tips.

Janson, Jennifer, ed. *Mosby's Pharmacy Technician: Principles and Practice*, 4th ed. St. Louis: Elsevier, 2016.

Jarrett, Christian. "The Psychology of Eye Contact, Digested." *Research Digest*, November 28, 2016. Retrieved July 16, 2018, from digest.bps.org.uk/ 2016/11/28/the-psychology-of-eye-contact-digested.

Johnston, Mike, Karen Davis, and Jeff Gricar. *The Pharmacy Technician: Foundations & Practices*. Upper Saddle River, NJ: Pearson, 2009.

Keates, Cathy. "What Is Job Shadowing?" Retrieved July 12, 2018, from talent egg.ca/incubator/2011/02/03/what-is-job-shadowing.

Levy, David. "Institutional Loans." Retrieved July 13, 2018, from www.edvisors .com/college-loans/private/institutional.

LiveCareer. "5 Common Healthcare Interview Questions." Retrieved July 16, 2018, from www.livecareer.com/career/advice/interview/healthcare -interview.

————. "5 Common Interview Mistakes You're Definitely Making (and How to Stop)." Retrieved July 16, 2018, from www.livecareer.com/career/ advice/interview/interview-mistakes.

Mayne, Debbie. "7 Tips on Proper Handshake Etiquette: Make a Good First Impression." The Spruce, last updated June 15, 2018. Retrieved July 16, 2018, www.thespruce.com/handshake-etiquette-p2-1216847.

Mayo Clinic School of Health Sciences. "Surgical First Assistant." Retrieved July 14, 2018, from www.mayo.edu/mayo-clinic-school-of-health-sciences /careers/surgical-first-assistant.

MedicalTechnologySchools.com, "How to Become a Registered Health Information Technician." Retrieved July 15, 2018, from www.medicaltech nologyschools.com/health-information-technology/how-to-become-rhit.

Moyer, Melinda Wenner. "Eye Contact: How Long Is Too Long? Research Explores the Factors That Influence Our Tolerance for Long Mutual Gazes." *Scientific American*, January 1, 2016. Retrieved July 16, 2018, from www .scientificamerican.com/article/eye-contact-how-long-is-too-long.

Muncan, Brandon, Nomrota Majumder, and Nicolae Tudose. "From High School to Hospital: How Early Exposure to Healthcare Affects Adolescent Career Ideas." *International Journal of Medical Education*, 7 (2016): 370–71.

Nurse Practitioner Schools. "How Do I Become a Nurse Practitioner?" Retrieved July 11, 2018, from www.nursepractitionerschools.com/faq/ how-to-become-np.

Ohanesian, Jessi Rodriguez. *The Ultimate Guide to the Physician Assistant Professions*. New York: McGraw Hill Education, 2014.

Penny, Steven M. *Introduction to Sonography and Patient Care*. Philadelphia: Wolters Kluwer, 2016.

Perry, Christian. "Sonogram vs. Ultrasound: What's the Difference?" The Bump, August 2017. Retrieved July 10, 2018, www.thebump.com/a/sonogram-vs-ultrasound.

Résumé Genius. "How to Write a Résumé." Retrieved July 13, 2018, from resumegenius.com/how-to-write-a-resume.

Rodican, Andrew J. *The Ultimate Guide to Getting into Physician Assistant School*, 4th ed. New York: McGraw Hill Education, 2017.

Tabloski, Patricia A. *Gerontological Nursing*, 3rd ed. Upper Saddle River, NJ: Pearson, 2014.

Salter School of Nursing and Allied Health. "6 Qualities Healthcare Employers Want in Their Employees: Characteristics of a Desirable Healthcare Worker." December 6, 2017. Retrieved July 9, 2018, www.salternursing.com/6-qualities-healthcare-employers-want-in-their-employees.

Santiago, Andrea Clement. "Before You Interview for a Medical Job." VeryWellHealth.com, last updated April 30, 2018. Retrieved July 11, 2018, www.verywellhealth.com/before-you-interview-for-a-medical-job-1736041.

———. "Physician Assistant Specialties and Salaries." VeryWellHealth.com, last updated December 2, 2017. Retrieved July 14, 2018, www.verywellhealth.com/physician-assistant-specialties-and-salaries-1736010.

———. "What to Wear to a Nursing Interview: What You Wear Matters." VeryWellHealth.com, last updated December 20, 2017. Retrieved July 14, 2018, www.verywellhealth.com/what-to-wear-nursing-interview-1736042.

Sarickas, Christine. "Complete Guide to Internships for High School Students." PrepScholar, May 2, 2018. Retrieved July 10, 2018, blog.prepscholar.com/internships-for-high-school-students.

Stephens, Stephanie. "You Should 'Work It': Networking to Open Doors to Better Jobs." Retrieved July 9, 2018, from www.monster.com/career-advice/article/networking-for-nurses-healthcare.

Wendleton, Kate. *Mastering the Job Interview and Winning the Money Game*. Boston: Cengage, 2014.

About the Author

Marcia Santore is a writer and editor from New England. She enjoys writing about interesting people and the fascinating stuff they do. Having worked as a magazine editor and writer, she's written on a many topics, including profiles of artists, scholars, scientists, and business people in a way that's approachable for the general reader. See her writing website at www.amalgamatedstory.com. Oh, and she's also an artist—see www.marciasantore.com.